EXPLORER'S AIR YACHT

The Sikorsky S-38 Flying Boat

by P.J. Capelotti

GW00771801

PICTORIAL HISTORIES PUBLISHING COMPANY, INC.

Missoula, Montana

LIBRARY OF CONGRESS
CATALOG CARD NO. 95-67578

ISBN 0-929521-97-8

First Printing: March 1995

ON THE COVER
"Sikorsky S-38: In Search of a Northern Air Route, July, 1929" original painting by Robert Carlin.

Courtesy of The Flying Boat Society. For information on how to obtain reproductions of this work write:
The Flying Boat Society, P.O. Box 1052, Abington, PA 19001.

Cover Design Mike Egeler
Layout Stan Cohen
Text Design/Typography Arrow Graphics

PICTORIAL HISTORIES PUBLISHING COMPANY, INC.
713 South Third Street West, Missoula, Montana 59801

Foreword

PETER CAPELOTTI's book on the S-38 has a special meaning for me, because it was on the S-38 that I had my first flight. I was perhaps seven or eight years of age, and the details are long forgotten. I do remember that my father sat in the co-pilot's seat, and I on his lap. The pilot's seat was occupied by the colorful chief test pilot of Sikorsky Aircraft, Captain Boris "Bob" Sergievsky. I remember the aircraft rolling down the seaplane ramp into the Housatonic River in Stratford, Connecticut. I remember that the water came up pretty close to the cockpit window as we taxied out . . . but since all was calm in the cockpit, I assumed this was normal.

As the engines went to full power, the noise was exciting. The spray across the windshield suddenly stopped and we were in the air. It all happened so quickly, that I was unaware we were flying until I noticed the water was below us. It was a wonderful feeling to sit on Dad's lap and look out the window at the world that was suddenly so vast and beautiful.

As I said, the details are long forgotten, but the snapshot-like fragments are still fresh in my mind.

To me, the S-38 will always be associated with my first brief flight. To my father, Igor Sikorsky, I believe the S-38 meant a great deal more. It was, after all, the first commercial success for the small and struggling company in America. It laid the foundation for the later creation of the great Sikorsky "Clipper" ships for Pan American Airways and so many other airlines and private owners around the world. In its day, it was the highest-performing amphibian in the world.

I am pleased and thankful that Mr. Capelotti has written this book about an aircraft so dear to two generations of Sikorskys.

SERGEI SIKORSKY, *Stratford, Connecticut*

FOR JIM AND EDNA SYKES
and grassy airfields and bright Cape Cod afternoons

Preface

IN THE SUMMER of 1984, as a graduate student in history at the University of Rhode Island, I happened upon a grainy photograph of a Sikorsky S-39 flying boat on display on the Quadrangle at URI. Soon I found another photograph of Igor Sikorsky himself, taken on the sloping Quadrangle in Kingston in 1934. Beside Sikorsky were Nicholas Alexander, Professor of Aeronautical Engineering, and Raymond Bressler, president of what was then called Rhode Island State College. I learned later that Alexander and Sikorsky were both refugees of the Revolution and Civil War in Russia, and that URI was indebted to both men. It was Alexander who had established an aeronautical engineering laboratory on the fourth floor of Bliss Hall, and Sikorsky not only lectured the students in the aeronautical engineering program but also donated dozens of items to the laboratory, including an entire S-39 flying boat, and the wing assembly of a much larger S-38 flying boat.

Those two historic images triggered an unpredictable and rather wondrous chain of discoveries and adventures. I located several Rhode Island graduates who had worked for Sikorsky and his company— notably Ralph B. Lightfoot, class of '35, who succeeded Igor Sikorsky as chief engineer at Sikorsky Aircraft, and who helped me found the Flying Boat Society. I immediately embarked on an "aviation archaeology" search and survey for these Rhode Island Sikorsky artifacts, so strangely vanished from campus decades ago. This quest led me, in an ever widening circle, far from the green university Quadrangle in Kingston—to archives in Boston, in Hartford, Washington, Chicago, and Minneapolis, on to an artist and pilot in Houston, to pilots in St. Augustine and Miami, Florida, then to a retired geographer and college president in Tampa. From there it was off to an abandoned outpost in northernmost Labrador, to deep lakes in Alaska, and to the blue tropical harbor of Fort de France in Martinique and, finally, back again to the green Quadrangle, and an important discovery: information about one Parker D. Cramer, class of '59, one of the first Americans killed in Vietnam and the nephew of the pilot Parker D. "Shorty" Cramer whose S-38 sank in Labrador in 1929.

Those same photos led eventually to this book, which is intended as a basic reference on one of the key maritime aircraft of all time, and which is planned as the first of several compact works treating the aeronautical technologies and maritime explorations of the inter-war period. To this purpose, this book represents my attempt to locate any and all relevant primary documents relating to the Sikorsky S-38 in the National Air & Space Museum, the National Archives, and in the archives of the Sikorsky Aircraft Company. These documents, as well as the most important secondary source documents, are listed in the bibliography.

Similarly, in order to facilitate the work of scale modelers, I have included many detail photographs, as well as a detailed description of how the ship was constructed. Many of the photographs were derived from the now-inaccessible flying boat papers of Sikorsky Aircraft Corporation, which I had the rare opportunity to sort and catalogue during an intensive student internship in 1988.

I have also listed, as far as it was in my power to do so, in the appendices, the numbers and disposition of all S-38s. One unique result of this research is that I was able to definitely establish that Sikorsky constructed 101 S-38s, rather than the generally accepted 111 or 114.

The book is divided into three main parts in an attempt to follow a dictum of the great archaeologist O. G. S. Crawford, who felt that obsolete aircraft were without question archaeological entities. Said another way, an aircraft cannot be viewed as merely an object of technological progress or inspired individual invention and operation, but must be viewed within the contexts of its time and, equally as significant, the natural landscape in which it was operated.

Since no S-38 survives in any collection today, and since no attempt has been made at a systematic archaeological search for one, I describe the S-38 as the object of *potential* archaeological inquiry.

Part One of this work gives a sense of the enormous spaces tracked by the S-38 and the times in which it was operated.

Part Two sets the S-38 into the Sikorsky technological lineage and provides a descriptive and visual blueprint should some future explorer come upon the remains of one of these aircraft.

Part Three returns in some detail to the complementary themes of time, technology and landscape. I describe a typical S-38 expedition, that of the *'Untin' Bowler*. I chose this expedition for several reasons. Being a newspaper-sponsored expedition, it was the S-38 journey that most intrigued me, and primary sources were available. Then, in 1990, in one of those mystic ironies that often mark archival research, I uncovered a photograph of the brother of Shorty Cramer, standing on that same green Quadrangle at Rhode Island, accepting a Bronze Star awarded posthumously to his own son, whom he had named after Shorty, and who was killed in Vietnam in 1963. (The ROTC Unit at Rhode Island has since become known as "Cramer's Sabers.") This discovery led me to Susan Duxbury, Shorty Cramer's niece and caretaker of the papers relating to his flying career and his dream of a Northern Air Route. These papers, combined with Robert Woods' *Chicago Tribune* dispatches, provided two primary sources related to the expedition, and when Alan Ruffman in Nova Scotia located Corporal McInnes' report in the Archives of the Royal Canadian Mounted Police, I then had three eyewitness accounts of the sinking of the *'Untin' Bowler*.

To these themes I have added an Epilogue that examines briefly the complex intersection of time, technology, landscape and individual heroism, mainly in the person of Shorty Cramer.

Finally, Igor Sikorsky, as an advertising strategy, called his S-38s "amphibions," spelled with an "o," to separate them from those living, mud-dwelling "amphibians" with an "a," even though the latter was the prevailing generic term for an aircraft capable of landing on both land and water. I have employed the accepted "amphibians" with an "a," but, since I don't care especially for either degenerative term, I have liberally interchanged amphibian with the more nobly derived terms "seaplane," "maritime aircraft," and, most often, "flying boat." I trust that aviation history purists will forgive this editorial license.

Sikorsky S-38 NC-8019, flown by the Curtiss Flying Service. UTC Archive

Acknowledgments

FOR THEIR CONTINUAL assistance and camaraderie, I would like to thank especially Dr. Anne Millbrooke and Ms. Mary Jane Carter, both formerly of the United Technologies Corporation Archive & Historical Resource Center in East Hartford, Connecticut. My student internship at the Resource Center for six months in 1988 was the direct result of Dr. Millbrooke's invitation.

This pivotal experience involved and led to many exciting historical challenges, not the least of which was the opportunity to accession, sort, clean, measure, and exhibit a unique collection of Sikorsky flying boat and helicopter engineering models. It also allowed me the chance to exercise my archival skills on primary records concerning Sikorsky flying boats.

There I met the son of Igor Sikorsky, Serge Sikorsky, the last Sikorsky involved in aviation. I also toured through the belly of the giant VS-44 flying boat with reconstruction manager Harry Hleva and his crew of ebullient Sikorsky retirees gathered together for one final flying boat assembly. It was also a joy to continue my conversations with long-time Sikorsky chief engineer and fellow University of Rhode Island graduate Ralph B. Lightfoot, Class of '35. I was given an office and a phone, which I used effectively to span the globe searching for survivors of the S-38 era.

Among the survivors I located were William Carlson, of Florida, who was a graduate student at Prof. Hobbs' weather station in Greenland in 1928 and 1929, and who remembered Shorty Cramer well. And, looking to lease a Grumman Goose flying boat for my own exploration of Port Burwell, I was connected to Captain Bob Hanley in Miami, who had flown the old S-38 Miami to Belize route for a fledgling Pan American Airways in 1930.

These experiences, however grand and irreplaceable, paled next to the sagacious advice and collegial exhortations I enjoyed then and continue to enjoy today from Dr. Millbrooke. Her assistant in East Hartford, Mary Jane Carter, also went far out of her way to aid my research and contribute to the feeling of good fellowship that warmed the Resource Center.

It was also during that internship summer of 1988 that I founded The Flying Boat Society, and soon after I received a note from Robert Carlin in Houston, awarded the Distinguished Flying Cross in World War II and one of the best aviation artists in the world. Bob proceeded to paint a series of Sikorsky flying boat portraits, which he then donated to The Flying Boat Society. His stunning portrait of the Sikorsky S-38 'Untin' Bowler, flying from a cove in Labrador, captured in every detail the picture I had carried around in my head for so long. Someday, hopefully, a patron will come to the Society whose similar generosity will enable us to reproduce this entire series.

During my searches in the Polar Archives at the National Archives in Washington, D.C., Alison Wilson was equally kind and generous. It was there in the spring of 1987 that we discovered a motion picture film, along with photographs, articles, and memorabilia, from the S-38 expedition to Labrador in 1929. Many of those photographs are shown here for the first time. Even though she has dealt with dozens of famous and storied explorers, Alison has the inestimable talent of treating even local heroes like myself as if we were Roald Amundsen just returned from the Pole. I also want to express my great appreciation to Susan Duxbury, who made Shorty Cramer's papers available to me, and who along with her husband Richard—himself a former Navy flying boat pilot—were such gracious hosts during my short stay with them.

Many thanks are due Alan Ruffman and, through his help, the Canadian Hydrographic Service, which sounded Fox Harbor during the summer of 1990, parenthetically seeking a trace of the sunken S-38. Thanks are also due Brendan McNally, Hollis Powell, Tony D'Aloisio, Bob Wilke for his excellent photographic reproduction work, Brian McCue, Paul Lagasse, Mitch Mayborn, Robert B. Hill, Frank Hepner, Armand Silva, William Leary, Col. David Dick, Larry Wilson of the National Air & Space Museum Archives, and former Sikorsky Aircraft flying boat men Ralph B. Lightfoot, Harry Hleva, and Ray Holland. Part of the S-38 in Labrador research was supported by a grant from the University of Rhode Island Sea Grant Program. Dr. William N. Still, Jr., former Director of the Program in Maritime History and Underwater Archaeology at East Carolina University, deserves my thanks for his constant scholarly and professional encouragement. As always, my wife, C. L., and our children, Jeremy and Jenny, were constant in their encouragement, their love, and their companionship.

Finally, I want to thank my editor, colleague, ally, and dearest friend in Kingston, Rhode Island, Professor Emeritus Wynne Caldwell, who has endured with me the many winters of the parajournalist academic gypsy. Her mystically practical insights into the meanings of words and the motives of people have mortised the imperfect foundations of my education.

Pan American Airways. March 14, 1927–December 4, 1991. *Rest in peace.*

Table of Contents

S-38 NC-8019, the fourth
S-38 built, which flew for
Curtiss Flying Service in
1929. UTC ARCHIVES

NC-8019 airborne.
UTC ARCHIVES

NC-8019 airborne.
UTC ARCHIVES

S-38 NC-9753, Col. Robert McCormick's *'Untin' Bowler.* UTC Archives

S-38 NC-8005, the third S-38 built. Named *Pegasus* and operated by J.H. Whitney as a luxurious flying yacht. UTC Archives

Inter-Island Airways S-38 over Hawaii. UTC Archive

PART ONE

Air Yacht to Everywhere

1 THE SIKORSKY S-38 flying boat, strangest and most strangely beautiful craft of its day, made several contributions to aeronautical history, not least the financial salvation of Igor Sikorsky's foundering aircraft manufacturing company at a critical juncture in its history. Introduced in 1928, the S-38 pioneered rapid and stylish executive travel, and its popularity provided the means for the Sikorsky Aircraft Corporation to survive until its purchase by United Aircraft & Transport Corporation in July, 1929. This in turn enabled Sikorsky to survive both the coming Great Depression and the rise and fall of the flying boat, and to live on as the pioneer of the helicopter.

In the nautical transliterations of the day (like "airport"), the Sikorsky S-38 was known as an "air yacht." When the larger and longer-range S-40 was rolled down the Sikorsky flying boat ramp in Bridgeport, Connecticut, in 1930, Pan American Airways founder Juan Trippe simultaneously enlarged the seagoing comparison by bestowing upon the S-40 the title "Flying Clipper." The derivations were apt. For private comfort and even a kind of spartan luxury, Sikorsky flying boats were surpassed by only the great dirigibles. In contrast to the airships, however, wealthy travelers and corporate officers found the S-38 faster, more convenient, and more agile.

The S-38 gave pilots the first large passenger-carrying amphibian aircraft, essential to the survey and creation of many of the first mail and passenger air routes. In that and many other capacities, S-38s were operated virtually around the globe, from the Hawaiian Islands and Australia, to Canada, Alaska, and Greenland, and throughout Central America and along the chain of Windward Islands of the Caribbean and across the Andes to southernmost South America.

"They flew as airliners in China," writes one aviation historian, "served with a Swedish charter line in Scandinavia, and with oil companies over the jungles of New Guinea" [1] (where one S-38 was sunk by a crocodile). And when their careers were over, and one by one the dynamic flying boats were retired, scrapped, sunk, or crashed out of service, it was believed, as Igor

Sikorsky himself wrote, "that these planes [had] made a total of over 25,000,000 miles, or roughly, one thousand times around the world." [2]

Like the similarly employed Dornier-Wal flying boats of Roald Amundsen's 1925 dash for the North Pole, or the Short Singapore 1 flown on a 20,000-mile circumnavigation of Africa by Sir Alan Cobham in 1928, the S-38 participated in and enlarged an interwar tradition of using flying boats for exploration and discovery. No machine in history was taken up so readily by the explorer and adventurer, delivering the first aerial filmmakers to Africa, the first flying family to Greenland, and the first anthropologists to study the Yawalapiti of the Brazilian lowlands, and no machine —certainly none in its relative infancy— so quickly overcame obstacles of geography which had thwarted terrestrial and sea-going expeditions for centuries. In that pre-airport world, or in places where airports would never exist, the S-38 became the way to get there, even if at times it managed to reach places from which it could never hope to return.

BY EARLY 1929, Pan Am founder Trippe had poised his company at the geographic and financial edge of a Latin American aerial empire. With proposed routes mapped and the complex intergovernmental negotiations to acquire the air rights to them well along, all that remained was for Pan American to possess a passenger aircraft capable of tying the system together. Trippe's chief engineer, Andre Priester, insisted that, with the lack of landing facilities in Central and South America, a maritime aircraft was essential, since "a seaplane carries its own airport on its bottom." [3]

Trippe agreed. He found the aircraft to conquer the piratical Caribbean Sea along the prosaic shores of Long Island Sound, home of the fledgling Sikorsky company. He required S-38 pilots to be college educated (aeronautical engineering majors were preferred, since they could tinker with the engines of their own aircraft if it were downed in remote territory), to be certified pilots, and to have a conversational ability in Spanish.

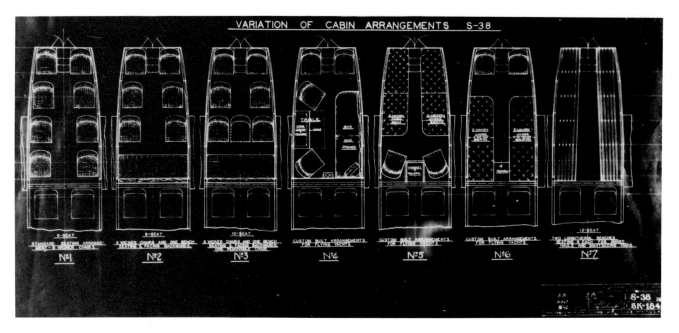

Seven cabin arrangements offered by Sikorsky for the S-38, including three "custon built arrangements for flying yachts." UTC ARCHIVE

Basil Rowe owned and operated a company called West Indian Aerial Express before he sold out to Pan American and became Trippe's chief pilot in the Caribbean. Rowe recalled that "flying for an airline wasn't the drab experience I had expected." He continued:

Pan American was growing fast and bidding for mail contracts over new routes, which gave me plenty of opportunity for pioneer flying. We had to survey the new routes to know what we were bidding on: the operating costs, the hazards, the time required for the flight, the facilities for landing. The usual procedure on a survey flight was first to send a staff down to the projected terminal by boat. They would locate the most suitable place to anchor a barge for me to dock the amphibian, and then would check into customs and immigration arrangements. When everything was ready, I would take off on the pioneer flight, sometimes with two or three company officials aboard. In most of the places we went into, aviation was entirely new. Most of the people had never seen an airplane. It was a big event. Officials of the town would be out in a boat at the mouth of the muddy, silt-laden rivers that riled the water far out to sea. I would come down in a flourish, starting up the flamingoes from the jungle shore, take the town officials up for a hop and there would be a big local holiday. [4]

Trippe employed Charles Lindbergh as a technical advisor, and it became Lindbergh's position not only to open ceremoniously the new air routes as Trippe acquired them, but also to contribute the image of

safety, stature and romance the public associated with his name. His first S-38 epic for Pan American, opening the Miami to the Panama Canal route on February 4, 1929—coincidentally Lindbergh's 27th birthday—typified the excitement Lindbergh generated for Trippe.

Leaving New York on the morning of February 3, the S-38 arrived in Miami that afternoon, where spectators and reporters crowded the flying boat and its famous pilot. Early the following morning, with 500 pounds of air mail stowed and secured, Lindbergh and three others, including Trippe, headed over the Florida Strait bound for Havana. Once in Cuba, Trippe delivered a speech and returned to Miami. Lindbergh refueled and continued on, southwest over the Yucatan Channel. He landed on the bay at Belize in the late afternoon. A tumultuous reception was followed by an S-38 tour of the bay for local officials, courtesy of Lindbergh.

The next morning, the S-38 winged over the Gulf of Honduras and Honduras itself—Lindbergh surveying sea and land below for possible future seaplane bases—before landing at Managua. The following day the S-38 set down in the Canal Zone at 4:30 in the afternoon, where two thousand people greeted Lindbergh. In the S-38, Lindbergh had shortened delivery time of a letter from Miami to Panama from eight days to three.

To escape the crush of press, Lindbergh retreated offshore to the aircraft carrier *Saratoga*. A member of the Army reserves, he became the first army pilot to take off from a carrier when he flew a small navy fighter back to the Canal Zone the next day. On the S-38's return to Miami, at the stop in Belize, Lindbergh became engaged to be married to Anne Morrow.

Later in 1929, the Lindberghs and the Trippes embarked on an aerial honeymoon in the Caribbean. Not one to ignore business interests, Trippe simultaneously blazed Foreign Air Mail Routes 2 and 3, south along the outer edge of the Leeward and Windward Islands to Paramaribo in Dutch Guiana (now Surinam). Along as Lindbergh's S-38 co-pilot, Basil Rowe continued on the route after the Lindberghs left the trip for a private jaunt to the Mayan ruins in the Yucatan.

The Lindbergh-Trippe-Rowe flight was not the first by S-38 to the outer islands of the Caribbean Sea. A year earlier, in December, 1928, an S-38 owned by Liberty Magazine made "the first air-yachting trip in West Indian history,"[5] according to the journey's pilot, Frederick H. Becker. A U.S. Naval Reserve lieutenant, Becker discovered that by landing a flying boat in a foreign harbor, he received an arbitrary and automatic promotion to master of a seagoing ship. Describing the lyrical feel of his blue-water expedition, he said ". . . I had to deliver a manifest, a crew list, a passenger list, and a customs inspection certificate in every port. . . . I came down in [a] harbor. Therefore, I was a ship,

and it was amusing to hand out a manifest and to sign papers as 'master'—master of an airship!"

The pirate ghosts supposed to guard untold millions in Pieces of Eight and Golden Dubloons buried along the sandy shores of the Spanish Main must have had the thrill of their ex-lives . . . when a great white bird . . . swooped down gracefully over their lairs in picturesque iridescent coves and inlets and landed with the grace of a swan on the shining waters.

The great white bird was a Sikorsky amphibian pleasure aircraft . . . flying over deep blue seas, studded with coral islands, poking our nose over mountain peaks and then dipping into shallow harbors, fringed down almost to the white and foamy shore with marvelous tropical foliage of every vivid color. . .[6]

Such romantic descriptions, as exotically hyperventilated as the stock market in 1928, would soon carry even more currency, during the long economic winter the onset of which was only months away.

THE GREAT DEPRESSION did not ground the S-38, which continued to be used for exploration

Charles Lindbergh, Pan American Airways star S-38 pilot, February 1929. UTC ARCHIVE

and adventure, although it did curtail full production of a smaller, single-engine spin-off, the S-39. Nor did the financial calamity slow the extension of Pan American Airways' reach into Central and South America and on into the Pacific, where the airline became a sort of privatized aeronautical branch of the U.S. Department of State.

Basil Rowe and Charles Lindbergh pioneered another overwater route in the spring of 1930, when Pan Am decided to shorten still further the Miami-to-Panama flight. In an S-38 stripped of all excess weight and outfitted with two extra gas tanks, the two pilots flew directly from Havana to Nicaragua, while a cutter of the U.S. Coast Guard stood by along the ocean air lane in the event the fliers were forced into the water. This "shortcut" became the new overwater record for a regularly established air mail route, abbreviating the previous Miami to Panama route nearly 200 miles.

The cutter proved unnecessary, though the flying boat was almost downed as it attempted to land amid a fierce tropical rainstorm over Cristobal. "It was raining so hard," remembered Rowe, "that [Lindbergh] could only see to land by opening the top of the cockpit and half standing on the rudder pedals to enable him to peer over the top, as the rain was building up on our windshield like a flood and it was impossible to see a thing through them. There is some advantage in having long legs." [7]

Greater adventures awaited them on the return voyage. Just out of Cristobal, the pilots felt the S-38 begin to vibrate. Neither could pinpoint the cause, so "Lindbergh passed the controls to me," Rowe recalled, "and crawled through the windowless hole separating the cockpit from the cabin. Opening the rear hatch, he stuck his head out into the slipstream and soon determined the cause of the trouble. . . . The horizontal member between the 'V' struts that supported the tail structure and carried the wind-driven generator had broken in flight, and the two ends were flailing wildly in the slipstream." Once again Rowe found himself grateful for Lindbergh's height. "With his toes hooked on the rear edge of the hatch, he slid along the afterdeck, and with his hands bent the two broken ends down against the 'V' struts, which prevented further waving of the tail section. . . ." [8]

Lindbergh and Rowe continued on to Porto Cabezas, and the next day to Havana and Miami, where Rowe extolled the S-38. "A lot we are asking of aeroplanes these days, to fly through all sorts of weather, across all kinds of oceans, swamps, jungles, plains, mountains, and snow-capped peaks; through rain, haze, fog, and snow; from hottest tropical sun-shine to coldest atmosphere at twenty thousand feet altitude and do it on schedule." [9]

The S-38 did more than survey air routes and fly mail and passengers for Pan American. In March of 1931, after an earthquake leveled Managua and set the city ablaze, an S-38 rushed to Managua Bay and with its radio coordinated relief efforts with other ships in Pan American's air fleet. Another S-38 airlifted the director of the American Red Cross to Managua from Miami. In September of that same year, after a hurricane laid waste to Belize in British Honduras, Pan American dispatched Basil Rowe in an S-38 to carry relief supplies, medicines and medical personnel to the city and its stricken people.

2 PRATT & WHITNEY Aircraft, the company that supplied the engines that powered the S-38, purchased an S-38 of its own. This "most luxurious" aircraft, with its dark blue fuselage and cream-colored wings, was used, the company explained, "for the rapid transportation of its executives in the ordinary conduct of the company's business; and at the same time . . . serves as an aid in practical engineering study." [10] The company had the cabin arranged as a small drawing room, with a full-length couch, high-backed lounging chairs, a shelf holding a thermos carafe and glasses and, aft of the passenger cabin, a lavatory.

Other executives, like *Chicago Tribune* publisher Colonel Robert R. McCormick, were also interested in the S-38 for its value in the comfortable facilitation of business. McCormick used his second S-38 to commute between his estates in Illinois and South Carolina, and to journey to the paper pulp mills in Canada that supplied the newsprint for his publishing empire. Robert Wood, the *Tribune's* aviation editor, described one such trip for an issue of *Liberty Magazine* in 1931. McCormick "lolled back in his seat, casually reading a biography of General Grant, from which he glanced up from time to time to look at the country unfolding beneath him. Once in a while he would jot down an impression on the flyleaf of his book. He was a veteran of the air who had traveled thousands of miles in this, his own plane, for pleasure and fast transport. He is . . . one of half a dozen of the country's leading business men who make the air almost their sole means of travel. . . ." McCormick's notes on the flyleaf would be quite foreign to any modern executive who "makes the air almost his sole means of travel":

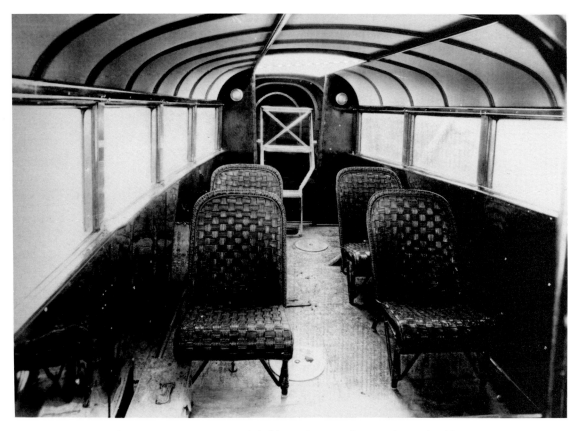

Interior of a passenger-carrying S-38, with ladder at the stern for entering and exiting. UTC Archives

S-38B NC143M, with the new sloping windshield and emblazoned with the eagle of Pratt & Whitney, flown by P&W in 1929 and 1930. UTC Archives

By 1932, Igor Sikorsky (right) had had his fill of trans-Atlantic publicity flights using his aircraft. Here he looks less than thrilled that George Hutchinson, in jodhpurs, is buying an S-38 to attempt the first Atlantic crossing by a *family*. UTC ARCHIVES

An early S-38 in Pan American Airways livery. UTC ARCHIVES

"10:30 A.M. We're now 10,000 feet up, and cold. The clouds stretch out to the horizon. . . The only danger is that we may be facing a head wind and run out of gas before we pass the mountains. Our fingers are stiff with cold. The drinking water is frozen and our windows are frosted.

"12:00 P.M. Red, the mechanic, has climbed through the window to get my altimeter; his collapsed at 12,000 feet. I must get more and better altimeters.

"1:30 P.M. We are now overdue in Lexington and must be causing anxiety. Now our motors are freezing. The right engine is missing. I think I see ground ahead. No, just shadows in the clouds. Ah! a hole and we head for it. Down to 5,000 feet, 2,500 feet, almost through. Out at 1,000 feet on the altimeter. If we had come down through the clouds we probably would have crashed. . . .

"2:15 P.M. A sign on a barn points to Washington Court House. Where is that? I cannot find it on the map of Kentucky or Tennessee. Oh, of course, it is in Ohio . . .

"5:05 P.M. We make a perfect landing in Grant Park Harbor, Chicago."[11]

For editor Wood, such adventures were nothing new. In aeronautical history at least, his employer will be remembered for sending his first S-38 off on a grand and failed adventure over the Great Circle Route. Geography and weather in the summer of 1929 defeated Colonel McCormick's scheme to pioneer an airmail and passenger route from Chicago to Berlin over Arctic wasteland. With Wood again along as expedition historian, the S-38 moored to a shifting tidal ice floe in a far northern Labrador harbor. The ice and high winds carried the plane offshore, where it sank.

3 NOT FAR FROM where Colonel McCormick's first S-38 disappeared, another S-38 met its northern fate. In 1932, after the Atlantic had been flown by a man (Lindbergh) and a woman (Earhart), pilot George R. Hutchinson decided to fly the Atlantic with his entire family. Undeterred by adverse press reaction to the announcement of his plans, Hutchinson bought an S-38, named it *City of Richmond* and recruited a navigator, radioman, mechanic and—as was becoming *de rigeur* for such outings—a cameraman. Hutchinson could not have known that the camera's film would become his most important gear.

En famille Hutchinson and crew departed from Floyd Bennet Field on Long Island on August 23,

1932. They flew to St. John, New Brunswick, that day. There, to save weight and increase the fuel for the overwater legs of the journey, the 500-pound set of wheels were removed to make the S-38 a true flying boat. The next day the expedition flew to Anticosti Island in the Gulf of St. Lawrence, where they waited out six days of bad weather. After the skies cleared, the S-38 reached Hopedale, midway north on the Labrador coast. So far Hutchinson had done as well as the *Chicago Tribune* flight of 1929.

On September 2, against the direct orders of the Danish Government, the S-38 flew the 600 miles of the dangerous Labrador Straits and alighted in the harbor at Godthaab, Greenland. Since the Danish Government had forbade Hutchinson from landing anywhere on the coast of Greenland, the transatlantic flight should have been effectively stopped before this leg. The Danes promptly slapped a punitive fine on Hutchinson, but did not stop him. He continued on his way 'round the tangled coast, reaching Julianehaab harbor, at Greenland's extreme southern tip, on September 7.

So far, Hutchinson had every reason to be proud of himself. Several more experienced pilots on the Northern Air Route had turned back or been forced down before reaching the point where he now stood. But Hutchinson was about to learn what they already knew—that Greenland had to be crossed via the ice shield, much farther north, and not around the perpetually fogbound southern coastline.

As the Hutchinson family left Julianehaab en route to the small settlement of Angmagsallik, on the eastern shore, fog closed in on the S-38. The treacherous shoreline soon disappeared into the mists. One of the S-38's fuel tanks sprang a leak. Hutchinson could go neither forward nor back. He brought the aircraft down at sea, fifty miles from Angmagsallik, and began taxiing for shore. The radioman sent out an SOS, and immediately a search was begun.

The S-38 began to take on water as it neared shore, so Hutchinson rammed the flying boat onto a rock outcropping, and all hands abandoned ship. They endured that night huddled together on the rocks, and in the morning light watched the swamped S-38 wallow amid the drifting ice.

Throughout that next day and into the night, the stranded expedition burned strips of their film to keep warm. During the night a random fishing trawler spotted what seemed to be a red flare. The captain of the ship signaled in to shore: "If you are the Hutchinson Flying Family, show two more lights."[12] Immediately two lights appeared, and in the morning the Hutchinsons and their flight crew were rescued.

Osa and Martin Johnson's S-39 *(foreground)* and S-38 over Africa. UTC ARCHIVE

Osa's Ark casts its shadow over a herd of giraffe. UTC ARCHIVE

Later, when the trawler captain complimented Hutchinson on the speediness of his reply to the trawler's signal, Hutchinson replied that no signal had been sighted. Quite unaware of any passing trawler, the marooned fliers, merely trying to keep warm, had picked that exact moment to burn two strips of film.

Osa Johnson (somewhat) safely posing aboard *Osa's Ark*. UTC ARCHIVE

Osa's Ark moored for the night on the African plain. UTC ARCHIVE

ON THE OTHER side of the world, above the plains of Africa, the S-38 saw some of its most stylized and glamorous service. By 1932, Martin Johnson and his wife Osa were already well-known for their land expeditions to Africa and Borneo, and the motion pictures they produced from these land and sea journeys captivated American audiences. But Martin Johnson thought he could attain even more spectacular results from the air. He arranged for Vern Carstens, a Kansas pilot, to teach Osa and himself to fly.

The Johnsons then visited Igor Sikorsky in Connecticut, where they emerged from the Stratford plant with not one but two flying boats, an S-38 and a smaller, newer, single-engine S-39. Specially modified for an African aerial safari, the S-38 had its passenger seats removed and replaced by "two light-framed but comfortably upholstered sleeping bunks . . . ," wrote Osa Johnson. "We had a tiny washroom, a little gasoline stove with two burners and an oven, a compact outfit of pots and pans, a set of dishes that nested into an extremely small space, and a supply of food staples. Every inch of space was used for storage, of course—under the bunks and seats and overhead . . . One unipod camera mounting specially designed by Martin was installed to facilitate his aerial photography, and I designed a very complete typewriter desk . . ."[13] The Johnsons ordered special paint jobs. Zebra stripes crossed the S-38, christened *Osa's Ark*, and giraffe spots covered the S-39, named *Spirit of Africa*. Their Sikorsky amphibians were fitted with supercharged Pratt & Whitney "Wasp" engines to enable operations more than 6,000 feet above sea level. The Johnsons hired Vern Carstens and Sikorsky test-pilot Boris Sergievsky to guide the two flying boats over Africa.

Like other adventurers, the Johnsons proved the value of Sikorsky designs for remote expeditions. As Carstens recalled: "There were no precedents and we were on our own: no weather reporting stations, very poor and inaccurate maps, no radio aids. We built seven different runways. . . . But the use of aircraft allowed much greater areas to be covered in the search for interesting things and people. . . .

The City of Richmond at St. John, New Brunswick. George Hutchinson in foreground. UTC ARCHIVE

The S-38 was really a workhorse, had seven hours' fuel capacity if needed, and could carry tremendous loads from all altitudes. We operated from runways and lakes from fifty-five hundred feet to seven thousand feet above sea level, and most always overloaded. We carried our own Tetra Ethel of Lead so that we could mix gasoline to the proper octane rating for our supercharged motors. This was necessary for both planes. . . . The S-39 had only 3.5 to four hours of fuel, so it was mostly used for the shorter, smaller jobs.

I think we were the first ones to operate both aircraft off of water at altitudes of sixty-five hundred feet above sea level. . . . [14]

Soaring over Africa, the Johnsons captured on film spectacular scenes of wildlife that would never be recorded again. Osa wrote, "Mountains, jungle, plain were a vast panorama beneath us; great elephant migrations, herds of thousands, also great flocks of white herons and countless giraffe and plains game were spotted one moment from the air and the next moment were being recorded by our cameras. We were able to land in ordinarily inaccessible places where white man had never been, and here saw natives of strange, remote tribes." [15]

At a camp on the Serengeti Plain, they set out bait near the S-38 to attract lions. From a base of operations along a small airstrip in a Kenyan valley in March of 1933, the Johnsons flew to Lake Rudolph, where they encountered a group of Turkana tribesmen. Thoroughly unimpressed by the flying machine, the Turkana did appreciate the shade provided by its 70-foot upper wing. Carstens offered some of the Turkana a ride in the S-38. During the flight he motioned to a cow below. "That is not a cow," the tribesman replied. "A cow has legs." Then the translator pointed out a tree. "That is not a tree," the Turkana responded. "You look up to see a tree, and you can walk under a tree. That is not a tree." [16]

Before leaving Africa, the Johnsons carried out flights to film and photograph Mounts Kenya and Kilimanjaro, and were joined briefly by F. Trubee Davison and his wife. Davison, Director of the American Museum of Natural History in New York, wanted four elephant skins ("just a trifle under full growth" [17]) to complete a display of African wildlife at the museum. Obligingly, the Johnsons transported the hunting party to the Tana River in Kenya, where they happened upon a large herd.

The honor of the first kill went to Mrs. Davison, who, recalled Osa, "took careful aim—I had told her about the little place in the forehead the size of a dollar which she must try to hit—and fired." [18] The American Museum got its skins, even if the kind of hyper-technological expedition that produced them would soon be as extinct as some of the wildlife recorded by Martin Johnson's cameras, or the *amphibions* that transported him throughout Africa.

At the conclusion of the Johnson adventures, their two Sikorsky flying boats had logged several thousand miles through African skies. Depression-poor audiences lined up to pay to see their motion pictures in American theaters.

4 CORPORATIONS employed their Sikorsky flying boats for more than executive commuting. When a subsidiary of Standard Oil of New Jersey, the Creole Petroleum Corporation of Venezuela, for instance, used an S-38 to conduct a thirteen-month jungle wilderness survey expedition: "50,000 miles without a forced landing." [19] In March of 1930, the Creole S-38 had become the first aircraft ever cleared out of the Port of New York for a foreign country.

After arriving at the rich oil fields of Venezuela, the amphibian "was used for photographic work, re-

The City of Richmond, aground on the coast of Greenland UTC Archive

The Flying Hutchinsons watch the star of their act slip beneath the ice. UTC Archive

Members of the S. C. Johnson & Son Carnauba Expedition, 1935: *l-to-r:* Al Schlanser, J. A. Hoy, Herbert F. Johnson, Jr., Robert Gardiner, and J. V. Steinle, with the S-38 *Carnauba* (NC-6V) in the background. COURTESY OF S. C. JOHNSON & SONS INCORPORATED

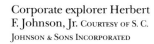

Corporate explorer Herbert F. Johnson, Jr. COURTESY OF S. C. JOHNSON & SONS INCORPORATED

Carnauba pilots Hoy and Schlanser. COURTESY OF S. C. JOHNSON & SONS INCORPORATED

Carnauba preparing to leave
Milwaukee, 1935. Courtesy of
S. C. Johnson & Sons Incorporated

Carnauba, front view,
Milwaukee, 1935. Courtesy of
S. C. Johnson & Sons Incorporated

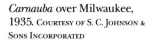

Carnauba over Milwaukee,
1935. Courtesy of S. C. Johnson &
Sons Incorporated

Carnauba at Dinner Key, Florida, 1935. Courtesy of S. C. Johnson & Sons Incorporated

Carnauba at Dinner Key, Florida, 1935; Schlanser *(in cockpit)* and Hoy *(on bow)*.
Courtesy of S. C. Johnson & Sons Incorporated

Carnauba in Brazil, 1935. Courtesy of S. C. Johnson & Sons Incorporated

Carnauba in Brazil, 1935. These photos reveal, perhaps better than any other, the size of the S-38.
Courtesy of S. C. Johnson & Sons Incorporated

connaissances, geological surveys and transporting officials of the oil company from Maracaibo to Maturin. This was a jump of 650 miles, which the Sikorsky did in five and a half hours. Otherwise it was a journey of from twelve to fourteen days by boat. With an aerial mapping camera hundreds of square miles of hitherto uncharted territory were photographed. Geologists were carried to remote sections and landed among the snakes and alligators to hunt for oil. . . . For more than a year the plane was never under a roof." [20] The pilot, L.E. Shealy, recalled that the territory was a dense "network of rivers, lakes and swamps—bad lands, like the gulf coast of Louisiana. The only thing it is good for is oil, and we found plenty." [21]

S. C. Johnson & Son, the makers of Johnson Wax, undertook a corporate S-38 exploring expedition in late 1935. The target was Brazil, where corporate explorer Herbert Johnson, accompanied by the botany curator of the Field Museum in Chicago, hoped to—and did—find new sources of the carnauba palm tree. Carnauba provided the raw material for the world's hardest natural wax then known.

Johnson, president of the company named for his grandfather, required an exploring machine like the S-38, since estimates for a land expedition ranged to upwards of a year. "To a museum or a university, a scientific expedition lasting a year is seldom an obstacle," Johnson wrote, "but to a man actively engaged in business it was entirely out of the question. I also discovered that it would be necessary to carry complete scientific equipment on the expedition, set up and operate a field laboratory. . . ." He further explained,

> After investigating and considering every known type of airplane, we decided on a Sikorsky twin-motor amphibian of the S-38C Type. This was the type of ship used by the Pan-American Airways on survey flights over the West Indies and South America, and the natives at all landing fields or ports were familiar with it. . . .
>
> To many, our expedition must have seemed like a great adventure. So it was, in a way. But to us it was primarily a job of research—the kind many forward-looking companies have undertaken in recent years. [22]

The expedition followed Pan American's Miami to Rio de Janeiro route, and rode "high above the clear waters . . . tinted by coral beds of fantastic, prismatic shapes," [23] as far as Fortaleza in the state of Ceara on the Brazilian Atlantic coast. From there almost half the carnauba wax in the world was exported. Johnson then turned inland on aerial surveys 600 miles into the back country, where he traveled at times in a Model T Ford converted into a railway coach on a narrow gauge track. The temperatures reached 110, and the corporate explorers skirted a revolution that had turned the Graf Zeppelin back to Germany before its arrival in South America.

Johnson's S-38, well-known in Brazil by 1935, found mechanics and landing or barge facilities at virtually each port of call. Even so, in the event of a forced landing, Johnson had a rubber boat installed in the upper wing of the S-38. It was not used until the return flight, and then only after a forced landing in a marsh north of St. Augustine, Florida.

Johnson essayed against American business interests that sucked the "earth dry of its treasures to provide necessities and luxuries for a lusty, growing nation . . . until industry found itself embarrassed by actual shortages of raw materials." [24] And he hoped that perhaps someday his own research laboratories would produce a wax as hard as that produced by the trees of Brazil.

On the return Caribbean flight, Johnson sat back in the cabin of the S-38 and echoed the romantic feelings of Lt. Becker seven years earlier. Dreamily he described "a chain of tiny islands, deep green in color, that rose out of a sea that varied in color from turquoise blue to delicate green . . . waters that once ran red with blood. Below us is the scene of century old combats between pirates and gold-laden ships of the Spanish fleet from Mexico. . . . We, with our airplane, could have used the islands for bases and made the old pirates look like a bunch of amateurs." [25]

The Sikorsky S-38, 20th-century conqueror of the Caribbean Sea, inspired many dreams of buccaneering—even on the part of a hard-headed, mid-western, Depression-beset corporate chief executive.

S-38s of Inter-Island Airways, Honolulu, 1930. UTC ARCHIVE

The S-36, used by Pan American for survey flights over the Caribbean. UTC ARCHIVE

PART TWO

The Archaeology of a Flying Boat

O. G. S. Crawford referred to obsolete aircraft as strictly archaeological . . .

D. P. DYMOND, *Archaeology and History*, 1974

1 IF THE INTER-WAR "Golden Age of Flight" produced the best pilots and most interesting aeronautical designs in the history of aviation, it also produced little more than economic heartburn for aviation industry executives. Orders for military aircraft had dried up after the Great War, and civil aviation concerns were not inclined to purchase new aircraft at a cost of several thousand dollars when war surplus aircraft were available for several hundred dollars apiece. Civil aviation at that time lacked both regularly scheduled air routes and the public confidence that went with them. Several small aircraft companies did manage to bring prototypes to market, but confidence in any new plane could—and many times did—fall as quickly as a strut could snap during a test flight and destroy the prototype.

Amid this scene, in 1923, Russian emigre Igor I. Sikorsky founded a small aviation company. Sikorsky had produced over 100 aircraft, including the world's first four-engined plane, in his native country before the 1917 Revolution. Fleeing the Bolshevik chaos, Sikorsky arrived in New York in 1919 to find his Russian work neither known nor appreciated in the United States. The Russian found temporary employment designing a three-engined bomber for the U.S. Air Service, but budget constrictions cancelled the project, and Sikorsky was unable to find steady work. Five years passed before he and a group of his fellow air-minded White Russian exiles raised the capital necessary to start the Sikorsky Aero Engineering Corporation. Work began slowly, and paychecks were issued at an even more glacial pace. As Sikorsky himself wryly described his new (ad)venture: "The greatest danger in aviation was starvation." [26]

At a chicken farm on Long Island, using cast-off

Igor Sikorsky stands next to a wooden mock-up of the hull of the S-38 amphibian. UTC ARCHIVE

parts and surplus materials (including angle iron of hospital beds salvaged from a local dump), the Sikorsky team commenced to build the S-29-A. The "S" stood for Sikorsky; the "29" signified Sikorsky's 29th design; and the "A" was for America, for this plane was the first Sikorsky aircraft built in the U.S. The even-

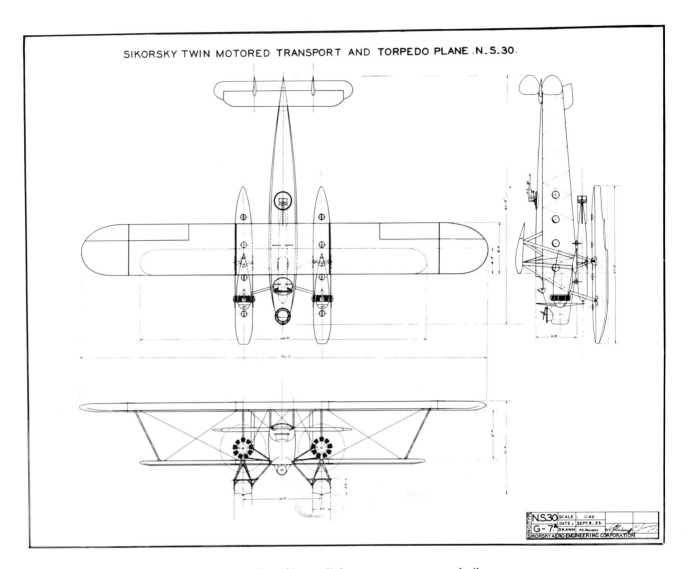

The S-30, designed in 1925 as a light transport, was never built. UTC Archive

tual success of this twin-engined utility transport persuaded a group of New England businessmen to invest in Sikorsky and his company, which reorganized in 1925 as the Sikorsky Manufacturing Company.

During 1925–26, the Sikorsky operation drummed up some business by producing a wing, the GS-1, that improved the flight characteristics of war-surplus Curtiss JN-4D Jenny aircraft.

The company also designed four different aircraft, each a single-engine sesquiplane (a biplane with one wing, usually the upper wing, considerably larger than the lower wing), designated in turn S-30, S-31, S-32 and S-33. These aircraft represented in part an effort to capitalize on the heightened interest in aviation caused by the introduction in 1925 of federal subsidies for air mail service.

The S-30, designed as a light transport, was never built. Sikorsky produced a single S-31, a small two-place open cockpit transport aircraft. Bought by the Fairchild Flying Corporation, the S-31 flew over the jungles and mountains of South America on photographic surveys. The lone five-place S-32 similarly went to South America, to the Andean National Corporation, a Colombian subsidiary of Standard Oil Company. This S-32 logged more than 40,000 miles as a company transport along the Magdalena River before the humid environment rotted the fabric wings and wooden pontoons. Next came the S-33, a small wooden racer. Sikorsky constructed two S-33s but, as with the earlier models, they did not begin to approach the kind of success necessary for the Sikorsky company to continue much longer.

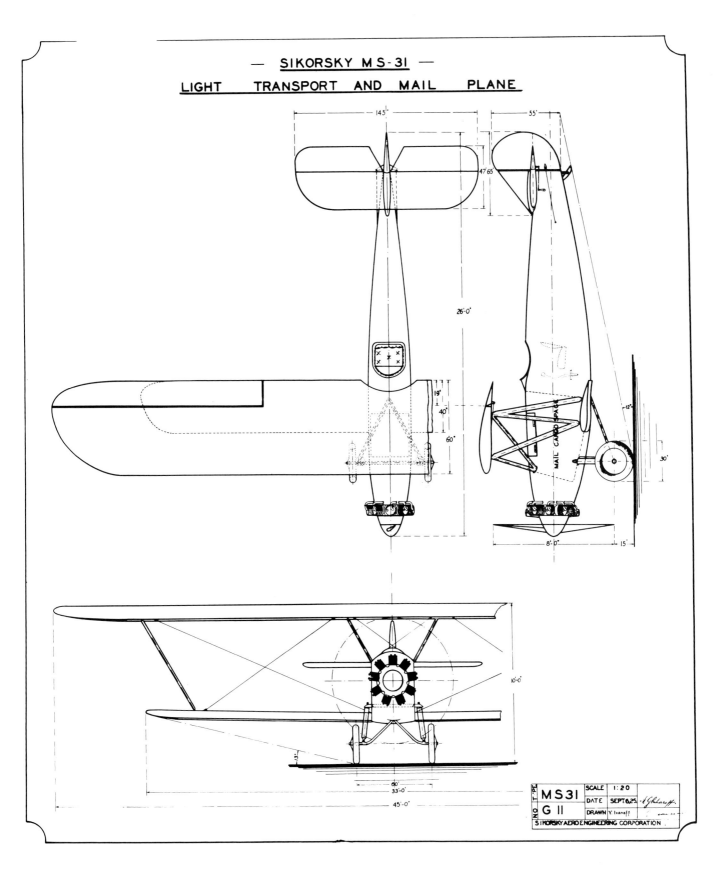

The S-31, a one-of-a-kind aircraft and the first of many Sikorsky creations to soar over the jungles of South America. UTC Archives

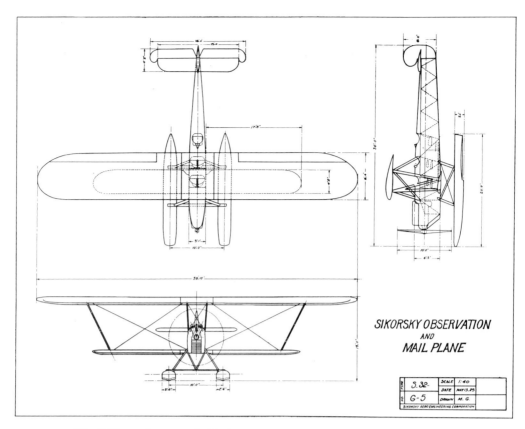

SIKORSKY OBSERVATION
AND
MAIL PLANE

TYPE	S.32	SCALE	1:40		
		DATE	MAY 13.25		
NO	G-5	DRAWN	M. G.		
SIKORSKY AERO ENGINEERING CORPORATION					

The S-32, another one-of-a-kind model, on the drawing board . . . UTC ARCHIVES

. . . and on the beach. UTC ARCHIVES

The S-32 emerging from the Sikorsky hangar at Roosevelt Field . . . UTC ARCHIVES

. . . and ready to fly. UTC ARCHIVES

2 SIKORSKY NEEDED a dramatic new design to capture a share of the limited aviation market, so he experimented for the first time with the design and construction of a small amphibian flying boat, the S-34. Before the S-34 reached flight testing, however, stunning events occurred that nearly destroyed the Sikorsky company while simultaneously revolutionizing air travel. Both events revolved around the race to see who would be first to pilot an aircraft non-stop across the Atlantic.

Against his better judgment, Igor Sikorsky in 1926 gambled one of his aircraft, an upgraded S-29-A called the S-35, on the transatlantic ambitions of Captain Rene Fonck, a French ace of the Great War, and Fonck's corporate sponsors. A prize of $25,000 offered by hotelier and philanthropist Raymond Orteig awaited the first pilot to fly non-stop from New York to Paris, and Fonck hoped to fly the Atlantic and capture the prize.

To finance the costly test program for the transatlantic S-35, Igor Sikorsky was forced, as he recalled later, "to accept advertising and publicity tie-ins with oil companies." [27] Pressure from these sponsors contributed to hurried test flights, insufficient preparation, and a departure date—September 1926—several

months ahead of Sikorsky's wishes.

The overloaded S-35 crashed on take-off at Roosevelt Field, and two crew members, one a Sikorsky engineer, were killed in the flames. The crash resulted in an uninsured loss of $100,000 and near bankruptcy for the Sikorsky company. "The future was again filled with gloomy uncertainties," [28] recalled Sikorsky. He added morosely: "The situation of the company had not been particularly brilliant even before that and by now it was generally regarded as utterly hopeless." [29]

Sikorsky—the man and the company—rebounded. Employees and Yankee investors rallied behind the man and his company. With confidence in the engineering that had produced the S-35, and in spite of the rushed and failed transatlantic attempt, the investors provided one million dollars in capital to enlarge and upgrade the facilities of the small makeshift factory. Sikorsky and his employees returned to work on the S-34 amphibian, and simultaneously built a successor to the S-35, the S-37, designed for another transatlantic attempt by Fonck. Sikorsky moved his operation to more spacious and modern facilities at College Point, New York. Located on the shores of Long Island Sound, the College Point factory had direct access to water and would enable Sikorsky to test his

The S-34, Sikorsky's first amphibian, under construction at College Point, Long Island, in early 1927. UTC ARCHIVE

SIKORSKY 6 SEATER AMPHIBIAN PLANE

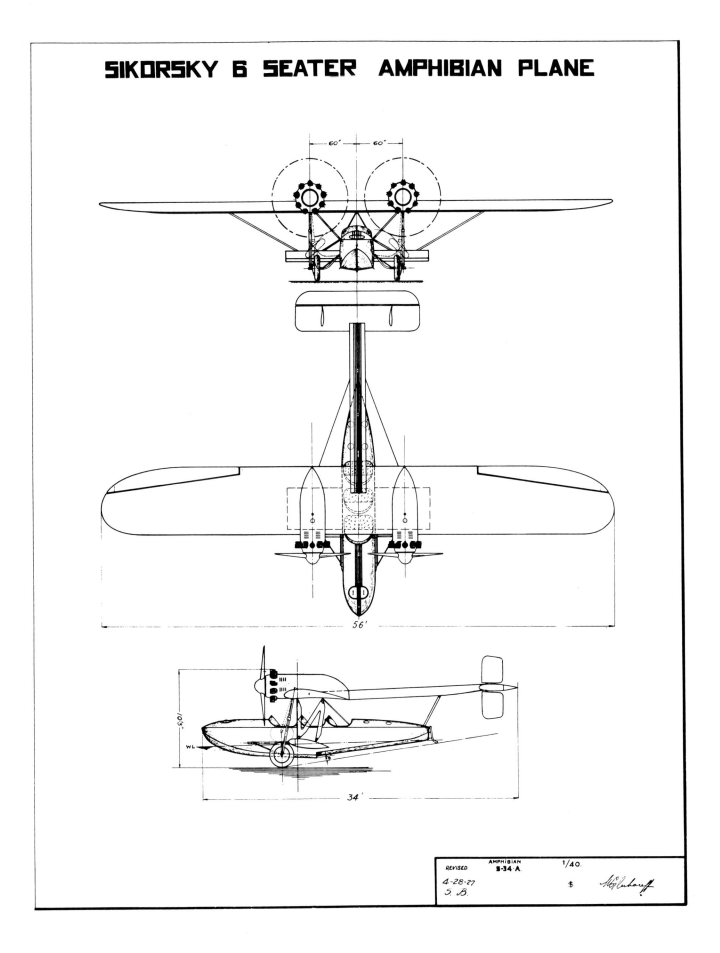

	AMPHIBIAN S-34-A	1/40.
REVISED 4-28-27 S. B.		$

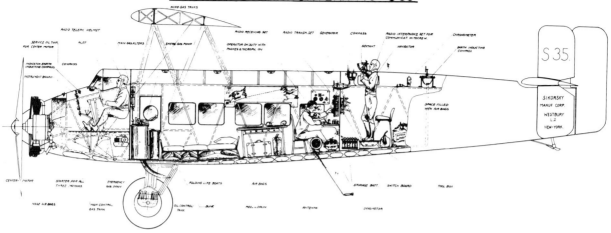

SIKORSKY'S TRANSATLANTIC —S-35.—

Design drawing of Sikorsky's trans-Atlantic S-35. UTC ARCHIVES

An exuberant and optimistic pair, Igor Sikorsky (left) and Rene Fonck, wave from the cockpit of the S-35 prior to the disastrous Roosevelt Field crash in September, 1926. *(Compare this with Sikorsky's appearance with the "Flying Hutchinson's" six years later, p. 6).* UTC ARCHIVES

seaplanes more easily.

Then, before the test flights of the S-34, on May 20-21, 1927, Charles A. Lindbergh flew non-stop from New York City to Paris and won the Orteig prize Fonck had sought. Lindbergh's single-handed, single-engined heroics electrified the lagging American aviation industry. The flight turned attention from European and war-surplus equipment to American products. It also ended the transatlantic aspirations of Rene Fonck. Sikorsky sold the specially constructed S-37 to a fledgling airline which used it to survey potential commercial air routes in South America. Sikorsky configured a second S-37 as a night bomber for the Army Air Corps, but failed to win a contract for production.

Unlike anything Sikorsky had previously attempted, the S-34, was poised to meet the many challenges of the new Lindbergh era. The small six-seat twin-engined amphibian proved Sikorsky's ideas for a durable aircraft that could both take off from and alight on land or water. It appeared to be an ordinary boat hull that sprouted sesquiplane wings and two engines mounted beside each other near the middle of the upper wing. Attached to the trailing edge of the upper wing were twin booms that supported the tail surfaces. This S-34 was the radical departure in design that Igor Sikorsky had been searching for since his arrival in America. The basic configuration dominated Sikorsky-designed aircraft for the next decade.

Until the S-34, no American company had produced an amphibian aircraft suitable for commercial use. Plainly, Sikorsky had studied his globe and recognized the obvious "geographical coincidence," as air historian R. E. G. Davies writes, that "almost all the great cities of the world, especially those on the routes of Europe's colonial powers, and the United States, in its overseas territories and its Latin American sphere of influence, were either on the coast or on or near large waterways." [30]

Sikorsky completed construction of his one and only S-34 in the spring of 1927. On the afternoon of May 31, ten days after Lindbergh's triumphant landing in Paris, he rolled the S-34 onto Long Island Sound for its first tests. Aboard were designer Sikorsky, who always put his life where his engineering was, pilot Captain Charles B.D. Collyer, and mechanic Hans Olsen. The flight was short-lived. Collyer piloted the amphibian to an altitude of 800 feet and, as the aircraft cruised along at a distance some 300 feet from shore, the starboard engine stalled. The amphibian spiraled downward and crash-landed in Flushing Bay near North Beach. "As the plane struck the water," the *New York Times* reported, "the trio managed to crawl out onto the wing and were saved by boats. . . . The

plane was later towed to the Sikorsky works at 8th St., College Point, Queens." [31]

The crash destroyed the one and only S-34, but not Sikorsky's commitment to the amphibian as the aircraft for his company.

3 CHARACTERISTICALLY, Igor Sikorsky calmly ascribed the S-34 crash to flight test experience and moved ahead with plans for another, improved amphibian, the S-36. Completed during the summer of 1927, this new aircraft differed from the S-34 in four particulars. The S-36 had a single tail boom, pontoons mounted under the lower wing, an enclosed cockpit, and engines mounted beneath the upper wing.

The new, lower positioning of the engines meant that on takeoff, props threw water spray into the windshield. This effectively blinded the pilot until the aircraft was "on the step"— hydrodynamically planing on the surface of the water and ready to break free into the air. Enclosing the cockpit protected the pilot from the spray.

Even with the water spray on takeoff (a problem that would nag all Sikorsky flying boats), the S-36 "was in fact the first American-built amphibian of significance designed for commercial use." [32]

Sikorsky built five S-36 amphibians—his first American (limited) production aircraft. [33] The Andean National Corporation replaced their S-32 with the larger S-36 and continued their water operations along the Magdalena River in Columbia. They demonstrated the worth of Sikorsky-designed aircraft in remote territory. The U.S. Navy bought an S-36, designated it the XPS-1, and tested the plane as a utility transport.

The fledgling Pan American Airways, beginning a decade-long relationship with Sikorsky, leased an S-36 on December 7, 1927, for use in determining the practicability of using amphibian aircraft on over-water routes in the Caribbean. S-34 test pilot Captain C.B.D. Collyer flew the S-36 on the survey flights. Pan Am thereafter became an aggressive sponsor of flying boat development, and remained so for a decade —until the appearance of landplanes and airfields triggered the demise of the flying boat.

Frances Grayson, a Long Island real estate broker, purchased the fourth S-36, christened it *The Dawn*, and decided she wanted to become the first woman to fly the Atlantic, if only as a passenger. To pilot her S-36, Grayson hired Norwegian Navy and arctic veteran

Frances Grayson's *The Dawn*. UTC ARCHIVES

The Dawn taxiing on the beach prior to the attempted trans-Atlantic flight in December, 1927. The flying boat was never seen again. UTC ARCHIVES

Oscar Omdahl. In 1925, he had flown one of two Dornier-Wal flying boats on Roald Amundsen's aborted dash to the North Pole. Grayson, Omdahl, a radioman and an engineer set off from Old Orchard Beach, Maine, on Christmas Eve, 1927.

Shortly after takeoff, Igor Sikorsky's grave misgivings about the wisdom of this flight were confirmed when *The Dawn* vanished without a trace. Five months later, Amelia Earhart became the first woman passenger to cross the Atlantic by air. What Frances Grayson did accomplish, albeit at the cost of her life and those of three men, was to become the first of many private owners of a Sikorsky flying boat, and the first to attempt to use it to realize a private dream of adventure and exploration.

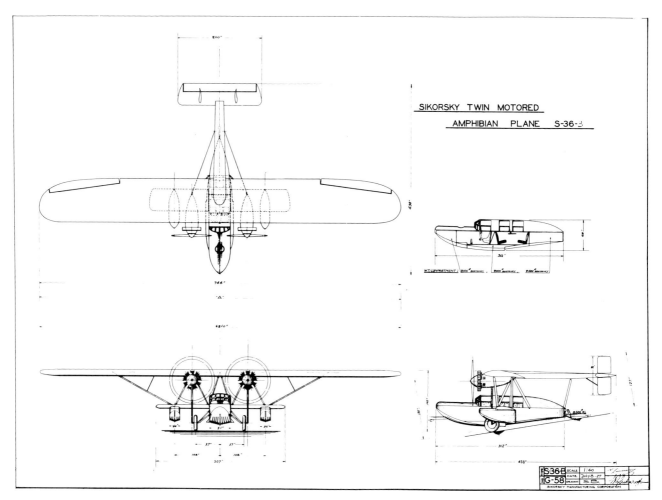

Design drawing of the S-36, Sikorsky's first production amphibian. UTC ARCHIVE

4 PAN AMERICAN'S senior engineer Preister expounded the idea that "a seaplane carries its own airport on its bottom."[34] When Sikorsky took this incantation to heart, it saved his company. The S-34 and S-36 amphibians proved to be the technical forerunners of Sikorsky's financial salvation—the S-38.

For the S-38, Sikorsky varied the basic design of the S-36. On the S-38 he used the more powerful 420-horsepower Pratt & Whitney Wasp engines, instead of the 200-horsepower Wright Whirlwinds used on the S-36. He refined control surfaces, increased wing loading (the number of pounds per square foot an aircraft wing could lift off the ground), and added new features like a fuel dump valve (his invention). He also enlarged the cabin to include space for eight passengers and two crew members.

What emerged from the factory at College Point in the spring of 1928 was a strange and brilliant evolution of Igor Sikorsky's genius imagination, one that catapulted his struggling company into one of history's major aircraft producers. His tenth American design

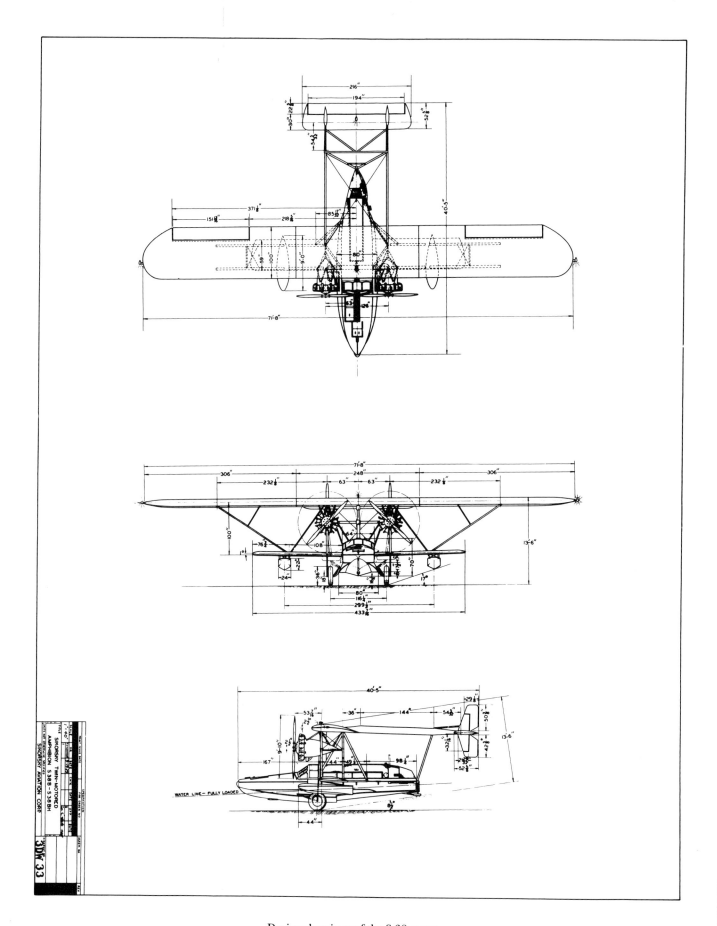

Design drawings of the S-38. UTC ARCHIVE

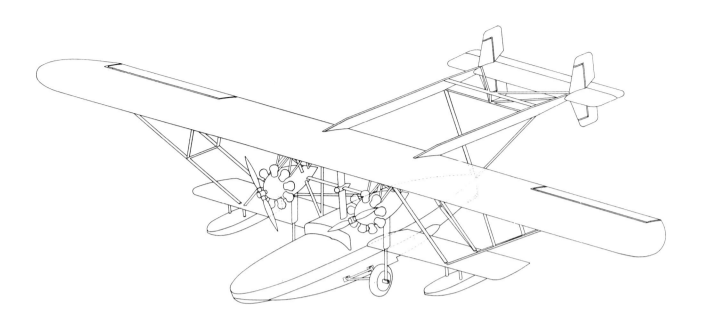

Early sketch of the S-38. UTC ARCHIVES

Diagram showing the arrangement of the cables leading to the control surfaces. UTC ARCHIVES

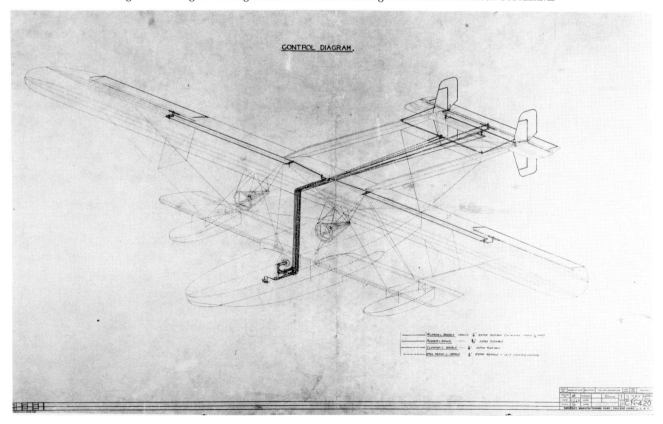

would yield 101 production aircraft.

Ungainly and large for its day, yet crafted on an intimate human scale—and once described somewhat uncharitably as "a collection of airplane parts flying in formation"[35]—the S-38 was made for water. A uniquely shaped planing hull and cabin were suspended between sesquiplanes wings, while a double outrigger reached back from the 71-foot Parasol upper wing to hold the fins and rudders. Everywhere you looked, wires and bracing and struts held the engines and control surfaces far out of the water.

The S-38 was crafted from a framework of oak and ash with almost loving precision. The hull measured 30 feet long by 62 inches wide, and the beam extended to 82 inches at the bottom by means of large stream-lined sponsons, which gave the hull better stability on water. Sikorsky covered this hull with heavy gauge non-corrosive sheets of duralumin, an aluminum alloy used on all Sikorsky flying boats. The sheets were riveted together and, separated by fabric from direct and potentially corrosive contact between the wood frame and metal skin, bolted to the frame with dur-alumin screws and bolts.

Several coats of preservatives and anti-corrosive agents protected the frame, hull, and deck. Inside the hull and on the deck were a coat of red oxide primer and two coats of bitumastic, a black tar-like anti-corrosive. On the outer surface below the water line, one coat of red oxide primer followed by two coats of bitumastic; and above the water line, one layer of red oxide primer, one layer of surfacer, and two coats of lacquer. A coat of bitumastic covered the wooden ash hull frame.

Sikorsky fitted the S-38 with his standard GS-1 air-foil, a duralumin frame covered with aircraft fabric. Sheets of duralumin smoothed the leading edge of all wing surfaces. In the upper wing, four ball bear-ing assemblies formed the basis of a double aileron control system, and maintenance was eased by inspection windows cut above each of the four assemblies. The upper wing and tail surfaces held navigation and riding lights, and the center section of the upper wing held gasoline tanks. An airspeed indicator and a rein-forced walkway for mechanics completed the lower wing.

The wings were given the same thorough corro-sion protection afforded the hull. Interior structural members of the upper wing, outriggers, and tail sec-tions received two coats of red oxide primer, one by dipping and one by spraying. The interior members of the lower wing were given two coats of the primer plus two coats of "special paint."[36] Wing surfaces were given two coats of clear dope, two coats of pigmented dope, and one coat of gloss.

As with the earlier S-34 amphibian, Sikorsky used the unique double outrigger arrangement that con-nected the tail surfaces to the upper wing. This double outrigger consisted of two metal spars covered with fabric and bolted to the rear spar of the center sec-tion of the upper wing and to the spar of the stabilizer. This was designed to keep the tail surfaces well above the water and at the same time keep the rudders within the slipstream of the propellers. Eight stream-lined wires and a triangle of struts attached to the very aft of the hull formed a modified box truss that kept the whole outrigger rigid. All of the major struts were formed from streamlined sections of duralumin, except for the pontoon struts and fittings and the engine mounts, which were formed from chrome mo-lybdenum steel.

The standard engines were two 420-horsepower "Wasp" motors built in East Hartford, Connecticut, by Pratt & Whitney Aircraft. Options existed to have the ship fitted with Pratt & Whitney "Hornet" or Wright "Cyclone" engines of 500 horse power each. On the S-38 the "Wasp" engines were covered with burnished aluminum cowlings attached in sections, allowing ac-cess to the power plants. The iron exhaust ring, design-ed to reduce the noise of the engines, was advertised as "an exclusive Sikorsky product . . . making the ship much quieter and pleasanter in which to travel" and enabling "conversation in ordinary tones . . . in the cabin."[37] Propellers were "Hamilton metal . . . set at the most efficient angle at the 42″ station."[38]

The fuel tanks, located in the center section of the upper wing, were also of duralumin. The four tanks held 82.5 gallons of gasoline apiece, and fuel was fed by gravity down to the engines below. Two inner tanks were equipped with "dump valves"[39] that allowed fuel to be jettisoned in an emergency. The pilot could ac-tuate these valves through a handle located in a paper-covered box above his head. To open the valves in an emergency, the pilot needed only to break the paper covering and pull the handle down. The tanks could be serviced via a walkway built into the top wing.

The amphibian used Sikorsky's first retractable landing gear, with wheels that could be raised in 30 seconds or lowered in 40. Two rubber tires with bronze bearings were mounted on axles hinged to the ship and fitted to hydraulic gears. These hydraulic gears were independent of one another, which meant that the wheels could be raised or lowered separately. In flight or when landing on water, an oil pump was actu-ated to raise or lower the landing gear, bringing the wheels nearly parallel to the lower wing. This same hydraulic system acted as a shock absorber for the wheels when the ship was brought down on land.

S-38 hull sub-assemblies under construction. UTC Archive

The flat windshield, a defining feature of the early S-38s. UTC Archive

The cockpit of the S-38. Note hatchway leading into bow compartment, and porthole above wheel to let in ambient light. UTC Archive

Interior of an S-38 hull under construction, looking forward from the passenger compartment to the flight deck. UTC Archive

Wheel assembly showing shock absorber arrangement. UTC Archive

When taxiing on water with one motor, lowering the wheel under that motor added to the ship's maneuverability. In shallow waters, the wheels could be lowered to prevent the ship from running aground on hidden underwater obstacles that might damage the hull. Only six bolts needed to be removed to detach the landing gear completely, thus making the S-38 a true flying boat. Pontoons, located under the lower wings, prevented the hull from listing on the water and increased the S-38's maneuverability on water.

In the event the Sikorsky-designed brakes failed when the aircraft was landing on land, the pilot was instructed in the simple expedient to raise the wheels and use the keel of the hull as an emergency brake. The elevator and aileron controls were located in a single box between the seats in the pilots' cabin. The wheel could pivot between pilot and co-pilot and lock in place on either side. The throttle and mixture controls, mounted on top of a control box, were accessible from either pilot's seat. Instruments included the usual altimeter, tachometer, oil pressure gauges, and a magnetic compass, all built by Pioneer Instrument Company (the ancestor of Bendix Corporation), and a Waltham eight-day clock. These were mounted in an instrument panel "carefully lighted for night flying." [40]

With such meticulously painstaking construction, it is no wonder that Sikorsky "strongly recommended" that a mechanic be employed full-time, preferably one who had passed "a short course" with the Sikorsky Service Department. [41] A mechanic thoroughly familiar with the Sikorsky S-38 should not be transferred from his duties "except for a very good reason," as Sikorsky Aircraft advised customers. "An average mechanic who is conscientious and knows the ship, is much better than a mechanic unfamiliar with the ship —no matter how great his skill." [42]

Sikorsky Aircraft went so far as to adopt a minor new advertising strategy, calling the new ship an "amphibion" rather than the more properly zoological— and more commonly aeronautical—"amphibian," to differentiate his aircraft from living organisms, in the unlikely event anyone confused the two. As a Sikorsky sales brochure cautioned: "Do not confuse 'Amphibion' with 'Amphibian.'" And though the word was discarded almost as quickly as it was invented, the company managed at least the temporary backing of at least one dictionary. "Amphibion—an airplane constructed to rise from and alight on either land or water. Funk & Wagnall's New Standard Dictionary." [43]

The twin boom tail assembly of an S-38. UTC ARCHIVE

Completed S-38 cabin/hull
being boxed for shipment.
UTC ARCHIVE

5 AFTER PROMISING consultations with the U.S. Navy and with Pan American, and though lacking guaranteed sales lined up for his new amphibian, Sikorsky gambled on a production run of ten S-38s. "Conditions were still difficult," Sikorsky wrote, "but somehow, by intuition and foresight, we were convinced that real success was not too far away." [44] He was right. The first S-38, completed in May, 1928, demonstrated "very good takeoff characteristics from land and water." Sikorsky exulted:

> It had a climb of 1,000 feet per minute fully loaded, and a maximum speed close to 130 miles per hour. The ship could cruise nicely around 100 miles per hour, and it stayed in the air on one engine. All these features were excellent for 1928 and at that time there were no other amphibians with such performance characteristics. [45]

A graceful refinement of both the S-34 and S-36, the S-38 was instantly recognizable wherever it flew. The prosaic, well-calculated constraints of aeronautical engineering caused it to look like no other aircraft before or since.

> The configuration . . . did not match the streamlined designs of today for rather practical reasons. In fact, several clean looking airplanes were in operation prior to the S-38, including of course *The Spirit of St. Louis* built by Ryan for Capt. Lindbergh.

It was realized that the hull must be of special design for flotation, stability, and low water drag. The two Pratt and Whitney Wasp engines and the Hamilton Standard propellers, tail and wing, must be well above the water. The supports must be as light and strong as possible. The experience of the Navy with the NC-4 and similar configurations also had some bearing on the S-38 design. [46]

U.S. Navy officials, impressed by a Washington demonstration of the new flying boat, ordered two, the first of twenty-two S-38s eventually sold to the military. [47] But the S-38 was not destined to become a famous warbird. In a remarkable turn, the Navy deferred acceptance of its prototype S-38, [48] so that the newly formed New York, Rio and Buenos Aires Line (NYRBA) could acquire one to open the first commercial air route in South America. [49] This and other new Latin American airlines and, later, world-ranging explorers, would give the S-38 lasting fame.

Pan American Airways, NYRBA's main competition, bought the second S-38 constructed by Sikorsky, [50] the first of twenty-eight S-38s to be operated by the self-proclaimed "World's Greatest Airline." The S-38 then embarked upon what Igor Sikorsky liked to call "the peaceful conquest of nearly all of South America for the United States airlines." [51]

PRODUCTION OF the S-38 began at College Point in the summer of 1928, and a new ship initially rolled out every four weeks. This schedule, it soon became clear, lagged far behind demand. "The first series of ships were sold out quickly," wrote Sikorsky, "a second series of ten ships were started, and also sold out in a very short time. Soon afterward the company found itself with more business than it could handle." [52]

The College Point factory was enlarged, but proved still unsuited to the production of large numbers of ships. Sikorsky reorganized the company once again, this time as The Sikorsky Aviation Corporation, raised five million dollars in capital, and in December 1928 purchased land at a site on the Housatonic River in Stratford, Connecticut, for a new, modern aircraft manufacturing plant. A large wind tunnel and an outboard motor boat for the testing of flying boat hull models comprised up-to-date aeronautical engineering research facilities. A dual roadway and flying boat ramp reached an eighth of a mile into the deep water of the river. "It was at that time that our organization

ceased to be a small one," Sikorsky wrote, "and became a substantial, excellently equipped, modern aircraft manufacturing organization." [53] S-38s began rolling off the Stratford assembly lines in early 1929.

The darkest days were over. Ultimate recognition of Igor Sikorsky's efforts came on July 20, 1929, when Sikorsky Aviation Corporation became a subsidiary with United Aircraft & Transport Corporation, chaired by Bill Boeing. A titanic aeronautical holding concern, United Aircraft itself boasted in 1930, with uncharacteristic exuberance, that it was in "possibly the strongest position in the aeronautical field of any company in the world." [54]

For Sikorsky, both the United merger and the growing success of the S-38 would stave off the coming stock market catastrophe. For it was the S-38 that, in Igor Sikorsky's own words, "proved to be the real originator of the Sikorsky Aircraft Company. For the first time it was possible to sell a reasonably large number of these ships. The total sales amounted to several million dollars, which was stupendous at that time. . . ." [55]

An aerial view of the Sikorsky plant at College Point, with S-38s ready for shipment. UTC ARCHIVE

Symbol of the new Sikorsky facilities in Connecticut: The test boat refines flying boat hull design on the Housatonic River UTC ARCHIVE

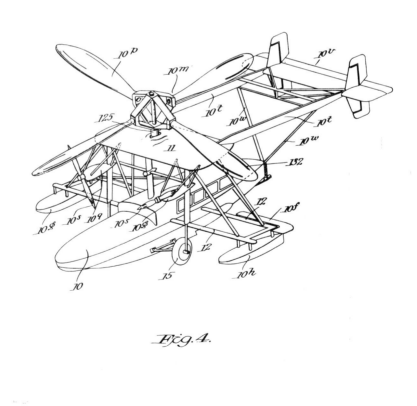

March 8, 1932.   I. SIKORSKY   1,848,389
AIRCRAFT, ESPECIALLY AIRCRAFT OF THE DIRECT LIFT AMPHIBIAN
TYPE AND MEANS OF CONSTRUCTING AND OPERATING THE SAME
Original Filed Feb. 14, 1929   8 Sheets—Sheet 2

Fig.4.

BY

INVENTOR.

ATTORNEYS.

Seven years before the helicopter: Sikorsky's patent sketch of a "direct lift amphibian." UTC ARCHIVE

6 AS THE VERSATILE ships entered service, pilots recognized immediately their many strengths. The S-38 could—and did— alight virtually everywhere in the world. As a flying boat with amphibious capabilities, the S-38 flew water routes for Pan American and NYRBA. It competed on even footing with landplanes on overland routes. With a gross weight of 10,480 pounds, ten passengers could be carried a nonstop distance of about 500 miles. Such performance could not be equaled by such estimable contemporary aircraft as the British Blackburn *Iris* flying boat, which with three 675-horsepower engines could not match the smaller S-38 for speed, range, or service ceiling.

On February 4, 1929, in an S-38 owned by Pan American, Charles Lindbergh inaugurated air mail service from Miami to the Panama Canal. Pan Am's original 90-mile hop from Key West to Havana had opened just two years earlier. Pan Am eventually flew the S-38 on routes covering 13,000 miles in Central and South America.

An internal Sikorsky draft document gives a sense of what passengers felt to be inside the cabin of an S-38:

> Easy access or exit to the cabin is maintained through a sliding hatch in the rear of the deck. The cabin, seating nine passengers, is large and comfortable having 175 cubic feet capacity. It was especially designed to give the utmost degree of ease and rest to the passengers when on long flights. A highly important feature is the fact that the cabin is absolutely clear of wires or members of any kind, there being a control box rising from behind the pilots seat to the upper wing containing all the engine and control cables. The cabin contains nine wicker chairs arranged with three directly behind the pilots cockpit and then three groups of two chairs each. Another important and essential feature is that the cabin is insulated against outside noises. . . . The interior of the cabin is finished nicely in mahogany and leather and the color scheme of red and black is very striking. [56]

Pan American equipped its S-38s with devices that, although in some cases a commonplace today, were unique in 1929 for the safety and comfort of passengers: radio equipment, roomy lounge chairs, full vision windows, wide center aisles, running water, steward service, and modern toilet facilities, "incorporated in the rear for those adversely affected by the air journey." [57]

S-38s soon became popular with corporate executives, who found that it offered comfortable transportation at the same time it cut travel time. By taking off from the Hudson River seaplane ramp in New York and landing at the waterfront in Boston, for example, an hour and a half could be cut from the normal landplane service between the two cities that required long commutes to outlying airports.

The abundance of lakes, harbors, and rivers along air routes meant that in an emergency the S-38 could land virtually anywhere. It did not have to search out landing fields in the fog or in bad weather. Any stretch of open water could double as an emergency landing field. Sikorsky was quick to point out that, in a 30-mile wide strip between New York and Washington, there were only 7.35 square miles of runway, compared to 550 square miles of water. [58]

The amphibian had advantages over seaplane designs as well, since a seaplane could be hauled from the water only with great difficulty. The S-38, by contrast, could land on water, taxi shoreward, lower its wheels, and waddle onto the beach under its own power. This made the loading and unloading of passengers less of the risk that it invariably was on water. The process could be reversed when it was time to take off. The S-38 would waddle back into the water, retract its wheels, taxi seaward, and take off. By lowering one wheel and gunning the engine on the side opposite from the lowered wheel, the S-38 could make tight circles on water and thereby increase its maneuverability in rough weather. A seaplane could not.

What was true of emergency water landings proved equally true when obstructions prevented water landings. If the pilot observed rough water, floating ice, or other flotsam that blocked his landing path on the water, he could crank down the wheels and bring the ship down on land. Similarly, the ability to maintain flight on one engine gave the aircraft an additional margin of safety beyond that possessed by single-engine aircraft. In areas of exclusive seaplane service, the S-38 could be converted quickly into a true flying boat by the removal of six bolts attaching the landing gear to the hull. The shedding of the 500-pound landing gear allowed the addition of another 60 gallons of fuel, with a concomitant increase in range.

These and other features built into the S-38 contributed to an appreciation of aircraft safety on the part of the public at a time when that public was still skeptical of aerial transportation. And, of course, increased public confidence meant more passengers for the airlines and greater sales for Sikorsky.

The exact number of S-38 aircraft finally built by Sikorsky has always been something of a mystery among aviation historians. Primary Sikorsky documents indicate, however, that Sikorsky constructed a test model and built an initial production run of ten

An Army S-38 (C-6A), attached to the First Observation Squadron. UTC Archives

An S-38H, NC-40V, outfitted with three-bladed props and operated by Sikorsky Aircraft from May, 1930, to March, 1933. This S-38 was destroyed in a storm near Hankow, China, 13 August 1935. UTC Archives

aircraft in 1928. Four more runs of 20 S-38s and one final run of ten aircraft contributed to a total of 101 S-38s built from the time of the prototype in early 1928 to the time production ceased in January of 1931. [59]

TEST AFTER TEST proved the superior performance characteristics of the S-38. In August 1928, the National Advisory Committee for Aeronautics (NACA) confirmed what Sikorsky had boasted of in the company's brochures. The NACA report verified that the S-38 in level flight with a full load of 9,900 pounds required 300 horsepower. With a total of 820 horsepower, the S-38 had a reserve of over 500 horsepower. Moreover, the S-38 could maintain level flight with a full load on only one engine, at the same time maintaining speeds over 90 miles per hour. [60]

A 1929 War Department report found that: "The response to control action and general flying qualities appear especially good when operating on either engine." [61] The War Department tests, conducted by the Army Air Corps at Wright Field in Dayton, Ohio, also discovered that the S-38 could reach a ceiling of almost 4,000 feet flying on the left engine alone, and almost 3,500 feet on the right engine alone.

The same tests found a few flaws in the design of the S-38. Accessibility to the cockpit was described as "very poor" for the pilot. Vision was extremely limited in every direction except straight ahead and, most importantly for the military, it would be "almost impossible" to clear the structure of the aircraft in case of a forced parachute jump. [62] The vision problem was not serious, given the limited amount of air traffic in 1928. The parachute exit problem was serious, and it contributed to a devastating crash of an Army S-38 (C6A) in California in July 1933. In spite of these drawbacks, the U.S. military purchased 22 S-38s—an even dozen for the army, ten for the navy.

SEAPLANE PILOTS, more so than their landplane counterparts, appreciated the qualities of the S-38. Charles I. "Sam" Elliot, chief pilot of Inter-Island Airways in Hawaii, logged over 5,000 hours in the S-38, and remarked later in life that: "There may have been better land planes and better flying boats, but none that combined the two half so well." [63] Vern Carstens, pilot for two years in Africa for explorer-cinematographers Martin and Osa Johnson, thought in retrospect that the S-38s were "slow and probably clumsy looking, but they had a great deal of utility that would make them very useful in bush operations today." [64]

Captain Robert Hanley, who flew the S-38 on the Miami to Belize route for Pan American in 1930–1931, remarked that the S-38 had problems during takeoffs. Spray would be thrown by the props into the windshield, effectively blinding the pilot until the aircraft was "on the step," and ready to lift off. [65] Other pilots reported similar problems. As Elliot noted:

In rough water or swells, due to the relative flatness of the hull bottom it had to be forced to stay on the water or it would porpoise before settling in, especially in long swells. . . . With a load, you sat so low in the water that props kicked up so much spray over the windshield that for the first part of the take-off, until you got on the step you had no forward vision at all. After getting on the step vision was o.k., and you were in the air like a scared jack rabbit.

The S-38 had very good landing and take-off characteristics on land. Getting into and out of small fields, I do not think that it could be beat. It had to be that kind of aircraft to operate in and out of the so-called landing fields we had at the start of our operation in Hawaii. On unpaved runways, and we only had one that was paved, the tail skeg was an excellent stopper. At first our two S-38s had no wheel brakes, and in a crosswind you had to blimp the windward motor until you had slowed down enough to let the plane swing around into the wind and stop. With wheel brakes this difficulty was eased a lot. One reason the S-38 had such good crosswind characteristics was the lack of a large fuselage for the wind to act on. We had some fields that had soft spots and when wet this posed a problem when taxiing, due to the high center of thrust and the wheels being set so far back from the nose. Many's the time the wheels sank into the soft dirt and the plane tipped up on the forward part of the keel. It often happened when only a few passengers were in the cabin or if it was empty. When this happened all you did was throttle the engines back and let the ship settle back—no damage was ever done to my knowledge except maybe to some nerves. [66]

Vern Cartstens, during the Johnson expeditions in Africa, recalls similar problems, especially that of take-off visibility due to spray.

The S-38 was a good aircraft insofar as landing and taxiing [were] concerned. It was easy to handle even in high winds, and I never found that landing was critical even under rough water conditions. . . . The S-38 was not a complex aircraft and maintenance was only normal. It was easy to service and unless it had been [in] water of a corrosive nature, all that needed to be done was to drain the bilges and floats, and open the hatches so that the interior could dry out. The S-38 was designed for easy accessibility in this respect. All wing struts were open on the end for draining and ventilation and the hull was of such sound construction that even under rough water conditions there was very little seepage. [67]

Basil L. Rowe, who piloted the S-38 on many of Pan American's initial survey flights of the Caribbean Sea and Central and South America, remarked of the S-38's hull characteristics:

> It had a rather flat bottom which made stall landings somewhat rough at times which is the reason that we [Pan Am] always made step landings, which is the equivalent to a wheel landing in a land-plane. However, if the water was rough or rolling such a landing was not practical and it was necessary to use the standard stall landings. [68]

The Army Air Corps operated 11 S-38s as cargo and transport aircraft, but the generally landbound Army pilots had trouble with water landings. Instead of keeping the nose of the ship high on landing, to eliminate porpoising of the hull, Army pilots were instructed to lower the nose, a practice that resulted in several hard landings, jolted passengers, and structural damage to the aircraft. After studying a series of such incidents, Basil Rowe commented that the crashes were the result of "gross amateur piloting from land-lubber pilots. . . . No ship can porpoise if the nose is held sufficiently high. As soon as the speeding hull shows a tendency to porpoise, lift the nose a little higher and it will disappear." [69]

The Army halted use of the Sikorsky S-38 permanently after a July 25, 1933, crash. On a flight over Oceanside, California, at an altitude between two and three thousand feet, the right wing panel crumpled and folded against the cockpit door. Even though all seven servicemen aboard were wearing parachutes, none could escape. Pinned inside the craft, all died in the crash. Later, the bolt that held the wing panel into the center section was found to be missing. That single bolt was the likely cause of the disaster.

WRITING AN historical description of a Sikorsky S-38 is invariably unsatisfactory. No matter how clear the remembrances, no matter how detailed the photographs, we are still left without the ability to examine the actual aircraft, with our own eyes. No example of a Sikorsky S-38 survives today in any collection, public or private.

If we could locate and examine one of the numerous S-38s that either crashed or sank, or perhaps survived alongside some remote South American airfield, what could it tell us? Could the archaeology of this flying boat tell us anything we don't already know from history? Can aviation archaeology take us under the surface of aviation history? If we could read the archaeological signatures written into its almost lavish construction, could we see, or infer, direct evidence of Igor Sikorsky's creative genius struggling to realize a vision amid crushing financial and technological complications?

With such direct artifactual evidence in front of us, questions would then arise as to why Sikorsky, even amid financial stresses and enormous pressures to succeed, created such a meticulously detailed maritime aircraft, when one might expect him to cut corners and rush his product to market. Were such construction techniques unique to Sikorsky and his band of Russian refugees, or would a comparison with examples from different American aircraft manufacturers of the day reveal similarities? If the causes can be traced to differences in "Russian" versus "American" construction, if we could examine examples of the entire Sikorsky lineage, would we see evidence that the Russian influence remained constant, or was it modified the longer Sikorsky lived in America, or to meet certain other exigencies?

Beyond testing the historical record relating to one man, examination of an actual example of an S-38 would, I believe, open up larger questions relating to human behavior in general. Why, for example, was the S-38 taken up so readily by those who, like the aviators and adventurers in Parts One and Three, exhibited an overarching will to explore?

Ultimately, we have to ask what it is that triggers the impulse in humans to explore—is it related to the technology available at the moment, and the landscape the technology is being asked to conquer? By examining the technology, by viewing the landscape, can we reveal the human motivation? Such questions loomed over two aviators and a reporter in July 1929, when their Sikorsky S-38 flying boat landed at an icy settlement in northernmost Labrador called Port Burwell.

PART THREE

Technology and Memory at Port Burwell

When at last we cleared the cliffs of Cape Chidley [Labrador] and felt the fine breeze and swell of the open Atlantic we were as men released from imprisonment in a mine; this stark wasteland was showing a disturbing reluctance to let us go.

DESMOND HOLDRIDGE, *Northern Lights*, 1939

1 IN THE 1920s, without a trace of self-effacement, the *Chicago Tribune* proclaimed itself "The World's Greatest Newspaper." The 1920s in Chicago, the city's "most flamboyant decade,"[70] were not self-effacing times. The *Tribune* was certainly the world's richest newspaper. Circulation nearly doubled between 1920 and 1930, from 436,000 to 835,000. Sunday circulation, by 1930, was over a million. Maintaining a war-time practice, the paper ran an eight-column banner headline each and every day, regardless of its lead story's news value.

The *Tribune*'s editorial slant, "combative, censorious, sarcastic, Republican, anti-labor, and anti-socialist,"[71] derived from its lord and publisher, the Colonel, Robert R. McCormick. A sharp-witted iconoclast, the Colonel introduced many of modern journalism's standbys, including the Sunday rotogravure color section. He was less successful in his single-handed drive for spelling reform, and even the *Tribune* eventually stopped using such neologisms as *telegraf, frate,* and *iland.*

As much for business as pleasure, McCormick owned several aircraft and loved to fly in them. He hated to wait for anything or anybody, and his private aircraft fleet shuttled him from lodge to office with time to spare. At times he would even take a turn at the wheel, though he generally left the flying to a hired pilot. He named two of his aircraft, *Buster Boo* and *Tribby,* after his bulldogs. English slang provided names for his *Arf Pint* and *'Untin' Bowler* aircraft. "He had asked a London hatter for a cork derby to ride to hounds in and had been informed that the item he sought was 'a 'untin' bowler, so if you fall off the 'orse you won't 'urt your 'ead.'"[72] During his lifetime he would own many aircraft.

Arf Pint and *'Untin' Bowler* were both Sikorsky S-38 amphibians, costing over $50,000 apiece in 1929, and the Colonel preferred them for their ability to alight on lakes in the wilds of Canada. There McCormick owned both vacation hideaways and the pulp mills that produced the paper for his publishing empire. Five of McCormick's aircraft wrecked, and he was aboard three of them at the time. But he continued to fly. As for the accidents, he claimed that he had managed to "walk away from one, run away from one, and swim away from one."[73]

Early in 1929, just before he purchased the *'Untin' Bowler,* McCormick was approached by a 33-year-old flier, Parker D. Cramer. Famous already as "Shorty," Cramer sought to renew his own personal attack on the Northern Air Route. The previous summer, he and pilot B.R.J. "Fish" Hassell had terminated an attempted Atlantic crossing via the Arctic with an unplanned two-week stay on the Greenland ice-cap, followed by a miraculous rescue. Cramer and his brother William had scratched out a living in the 1920s as barnstormers, flying under bridges, making barely survivable parachute jumps, and selling war-surplus parts for Curtiss JN-4 Jennys.[74] Inspired by the commercial possibilities of a transatlantic air route that covered more land than ocean, Cramer had sworn his life to its development and exploitation.

By 1929, there had been only one successful round-trip flight between Europe and the United States, that of the R-34 dirigible in 1919.[75] Aircraft, still in their relative infancy, were limited to making short hops, from New York to Boston, Boston to Nova Scotia, Nova Scotia to Greenland, and so on, across to

Europe. New York was the favored terminus for these sea hops, as it had been for Shorty Cramer's midwestern rival, Charles Lindbergh, when Lindbergh flew the Atlantic nonstop and solo in 1927. But Lindbergh carried no payload, and flew a specially modified plane. Cramer sought to use essentially off-the-shelf technology on a different route—with land stops—to establish a regular, passenger-carrying airline across the North Atlantic.

The Great Circle distance (the shortest arc between two points on a globe) separating Newfoundland from Ireland was nearly 2,000 miles, and that was the most direct ocean crossing with land stops. But no aircraft existed that could take a payload that far, and in any case the weather over that stretch was horrendous at best, with disastrous fogs around Newfoundland and vicious prevailing westerly winds, making a return trip from Europe a continuous battle.

Cramer, almost single-handedly, sought to build his air bridge north of the bad weather, and he was well aware that the S-38 was the only sea-going aircraft of its day that could make the 500-mile hops to Europe with any appreciable amount of payload. Thus he turned to McCormick. Cramer's northern route, as he himself wrote, was "several hundred miles shorter between important cities of America and Europe than the proposed Southern Route Via Bermuda and the Azores. . . . The payload of existing aircraft in a jump of 2,000 miles, as is required on the water route, is so greatly reduced as to make the usefulness of the line practically negligible. The Northern Route, with no jump exceeding 500 miles, will permit existing planes to carry normal payloads of profitable size." [76]

The difficulties to be encountered in establishing a North Atlantic air route were enormous. No infrastructure existed to handle land aircraft or support them once on the ground, and where open water existed for flying boat operations there were no marked channels, no channel sweeping equipment, and no loading gear, and no accommodations for pilots or passengers. If Cramer's plan had one obvious flaw, it was that the aircraft itself was only one aspect of any air operation.

Cramer understood this, but, without a financier behind him, he was powerless to change it. He was attempting to establish a regular transatlantic airline using the only technology and geography that existed for him in 1929. The kind of blue-water flying boat that could span the Atlantic would not roll out of Igor Sikorsky's workshop until three years after Shorty Cramer vanished over the North Sea.

Cramer envisioned an infrastructure where it was needed most, above 55 degrees north, just north of some of the worst climatic and weather conditions in the world. Only as late as April, 1928, had an airplane crossed the Atlantic from east to west. The Junkers W33 Bremen completed the crossing from Ireland to Greely Island, off Labrador. An international encyclopedia describes the situation then: "As early as 1928 Pan American Airways began investigating possible North Atlantic routes. Numerous surveys were made, including one by Lindbergh, who studied a northern route via Greenland and Iceland, making his flight in a Lockheed Sirius seaplane. The very big problem was aircraft range, and Pan American and Imperial Airways did not begin trial flights until 1937" [with the long-range, four-engined Sikorsky S-42.] [77]

As Cramer himself wrote: "The proposed route is north of the dangerous fog and storm area of the North Atlantic [and] by crossing Greenland at two different levels it will be possible to come in with a tail wind at high levels and go out at lower levels with a tail wind." [78]

MCCORMICK, THOUGH watchful of his money (he once fired a correspondent who turned in a bill of $20,000 for a foreign trip, the only purpose of which was to fulfill a promise the correspondent had made to his mother to one day send her a post card from Timbuktu), almost certainly looked upon the proposed S-38 journey as little more than a highly speculatively circulation promotion stunt using his own private aircraft.

Such stunts were nothing new. Already in the 1920s, newspapers had resorted to printing lottery tickets, giving cash prizes to winners. Competitor papers countered with bigger lotteries and prizes. Despite their dubious legality, these promotions were taken to new heights in Chicago, where sales of the *Tribune* skyrocketed. When the government shut the lotteries down, the *Tribune* turned to new areas of promotion, including extended sports coverage in both the paper and over the *Tribune*-owned radio station, WGN. Coverage on international events was handled by their own cadre of foreign correspondents, including William S. Shirer and George Seldes.

With the popularity of aviators and their exploits at an all-time high after the transatlantic epic of Lindbergh, it seemed only natural to McCormick to combine his own aeronautical passion with that of the public. In Parker Cramer, he had a famous aviator who had held the world stage for two weeks in August and September of 1928 during his disappearance over Greenland. The Colonel, who was also known as a "notorious optimist on weather conditions,"[79] adopted Cramer's plan as his own: to send his Sikorsky S-38 off on the uncharted Great Circle Route to Europe, to fly round-trip from the New World to the Old and back again to become the first in the world to do so.

By convincing McCormick to sponsor a Chicago entry into the efforts to create international air routes, Cramer could accomplish what one of the *Tribune*'s lotteries could not: create Chicago as an international city. McCormick and the *Tribune* could pioneer an air-mail and passenger route between Chicago and Berlin. The Colonel could also pioneer a new era in world travel, north over the northern Quebec wastes, over Remi Lake, Rupert House, and Port Burwell. On to Greenland, Iceland, Norway, and Berlin. It could, as the *Tribune*'s Pulitzer Prize-winning cartoonist John T. McCutcheon prophesied, help Canada in opening parts of its vast "waste" territories. [80]

And, of course, it wouldn't hurt newspaper sales.

To accomplish his goal, the owner of the richest newspaper in the world turned in March, 1929, to Igor Sikorsky, owner of a company that had barely survived 1928.

A. LOT OF ADVENTURESOME YOUTHS LIKE TO STOW AWAY

"A Lot of Adventuresome Youths Like to Stow Away," by McCutcheon, *Chicago Tribune*, July 2, 1929. Courtesy of *Chicago Tribune*

2 IN JUNE OF 1929, McCormick bought S-38-B 114-1, the eleventh S-38 produced at the Sikorsky plant at College Point, Long Island. Registered as NC-9753, powered by two 450-horsepower Pratt & Whitney Wasp engines, McCormick's S-38 received special modifications for the Colonel's planned transatlantic run. The cabin accommodations were removed and replaced by three 100-gallon fuel tanks, an expediency necessitated by the lack of infrastructure along the planned route. If the route proved successful, the infrastructure would grow so that planes could follow the route with passengers and cargo, not extra fuel tanks.

When these changes were in place, on June 28, 1929, the big air yacht was rolled down the gangway at Astoria, Long Island, and into the waters of Flushing Bay. Pilot Robert H. Gast was at the controls. Gast, born in Louisville, Kentucky, in 1896, had flown for the Canadian contingent of the Royal Flying Corps during the Great War, and in the 1920s had worked for the Aeronautical Branch of the Department of Commerce.

In the cabin at the radio was Shorty Cramer, the co-pilot, navigator, and radioman. Born in 1896 in Lafayette, Indiana, Cramer at the age of 19 had joined the Curtiss Company and, like Gast, he had worked for a short time in the Department of Commerce. In August 1928, Cramer had flown with Bert R. J. Hassell in the Stinson monoplane *City of Rockford*, from Rockford, Illinois, to a forced landing in Greenland, where the flight came to a cold and ignominious end. Their resulting two-week trek across the ice cap and re-emergence after being given up for dead, had made them both famous. In April 1929, Cramer had followed up the Greenland adventure with a flawless survey flight in a Cessna monoplane from Nome, Alaska, over the Siberian wastes and back to Nome, then to New York. Soon afterwards, he had his meeting with the Colonel.

The plan was to fly from Astoria to Cleveland to Chicago, and from Chicago to launch the historic flying boat toward Berlin. Flipping on the electric starter, Gast gunned the engines. The S-38, reported McCormick's *Tribune*: "rose from the white capped waters of Flushing Bay as gracefully as a sea gull, despite her load of almost 10,000 pounds . . .

The *'Untin' Bowler (foreground)* ready to leave the Sikorsky plant at College Point, March, 1929. UTC ARCHIVE

It was 2:18 p.m. when the *Bowler* lifted clear of the water after a 1,000 foot dash through the bay that sent a curtain of spray flying so high it almost hid the boat. She rose like a shot to 1,000 feet, circled back of North Beach and dived low over the crowd that lined the pier. Gast leaned from his seat to wave goodby to the brother pilots who had come up the bay to see him off on his long flight.

A moment later, as he was climbing over the bay, he waved to Frank T. Courtney, the British pilot, who once tried a trans-Atlantic hop, as Courtney sat riding the waves in his seaplane far below the *Bowler*. Then the great gray Sikorsky flashed on toward the skyscrapers of Manhattan, turned north into the Hudson River valley, and set its course for Albany.

The *Bowler* monopolized attention at the tidy airport—which is more like an exclusive yacht club than it is a flying field—from the time the first spectators arrived this morning, attracted by stories in the newspapers of the coming round trip flight to Berlin. A crowd gathered about the ship as the mechanics and radio men began their final inspection. The radio men were sleepy-eyed, for they had worked until early morning hooking up the instrument that is going to keep the *Bowler* in constant communication with the *Chicago Tribune* during its days on the unplotted far northern course. [81]

Cramer and Gast were both hounded for interviews before the S-38 left Flushing Bay, and both exuded the confidence of the age.

Gast: "The worst part of the whole trip is over— the waiting here in New York. There were a million things to do. From now on it ought to be easy sailing. We've got the right ship, the right maps, supplies every eight hundred miles, and I'll bet you $20 right now that Shorty Cramer and I hop right over there and home again with no trouble." [82]

Cramer: "Sure, we'll make it right on schedule. We are going to fly as straight to Berlin and back as we are to Cleveland this afternoon. The only thing that can hold us back is the weather and when there is good weather in the Arctic, it usually is good for a week or more. There will be a new mail route from Chicago to Berlin when we get back. I was up as far as Prof. Hobb's camp [in Greenland] last summer when Bert Hassel and I attempted a flight similar to this one. This time, however, we have planned further ahead, and we are making shorter jumps. We'll get there and back O.K." [83]

At 7:09 that night, the S-38 dropped from a smoky sky and landed at the Buffalo Municipal Airport. After fighting a 40 miles per hour headwind up the Hudson River from Astoria and down the Mohawk Valley to Buffalo, Gast decided to recuperate overnight at

Buffalo rather than chance their original destination of Cleveland. Gast told reporters that people had turned out all along the route to see the S-38: "Several places the roofs of factories and office buildings were dotted with people who had come out to wave to us." [84]

The improvised stop in Buffalo became typical of the flight, so the *Tribune*, as did all newspapers sponsoring such expeditions, took great pains to portray the journey as something more than a mere aeronautical promotional stunt. "It will be a scientific survey of the most logical air path between the old and the new worlds," [85] the *Tribune* with requisite gravity told its readers on Saturday, June 29, 1929, in its usual eight column front page banner. The flight of the *'Untin' Bowler*, as Shorty Cramer's scientific survey, took on the genuine significance that the *Tribune*, in its marvelously detailed explanations, sought so vigorously to announce.

Its aim is to demonstrate that Chicago is the natural and the best terminus for an airline to Europe and that the northern circle, with land most of the way, offers fewer hazards than any other lane.

It expects to show the practicability of a terminal in the industrial center of the United States, from which planes could be dispatched to and received from central Europe. Feeder lines already radiate out of Chicago making direct connections with Mexico and Central America, and a five day hookup for mail service between Central America and Europe is possible.

. . . the distance from Chicago to the mainland of Europe, because of the spherical nature of the earth's surface, is less than 200 miles farther than the distance from New York to the European mainland.

. . . bases already have been established every eight hundred miles along the route and could be set up every 400 miles along 50 percent of the course. The cost of bases every 400 miles would be less than the expense of establishing one of the proposed "floating islands" in the Atlantic [the Armstrong Seadrome, discussed later].

Thus the longest hop on the northern route can be made on six hours fuel, while the other way 30 hours is the minimum. This gives the great circle a payload possibility, feasible in the summer under existing conditions, over which a ship can fly and still keep within the load limits allowed by the department of commerce. The other way gasoline alone far exceeds the load limit. [86]

On June 30, 1929, the S-38 plowed its way to Chicago amid the worst electrical storm of the season. Gales rocked the ship nearly all the way from Buffalo. En route, in the back of the cabin, Shorty Cramer ran tests on the short-wave radio that would keep the S-38 in contact with Tribune Tower in Chicago. Once the ship disappeared into the Arctic mists, this would be its only link with the rest of the world. The big craft appeared out of the dark sky along the south shore of Lake Michigan in the late afternoon, made a pass over Milwaukee—where the city greeted its fly-by with "sirens, whistles, and cheers," [87] and landed back at Chicago at 7:10 p.m. Five hundred spectators waited there in the rain for a glimpse of Colonel McCormick's air yacht.

In Chicago, Gast and Cramer were joined by Robert W. Wood, the Tribune's aviation editor whom McCormick assigned as flight correspondent and expedition historian. The three men posed for Tribune photographers while the S-38 received last minute engine checks and McCormick went on his own radio station with an editorial proclaiming the virtues of the flight. Visitors by the hundreds streamed in to stare at the big Sikorsky.

While McCormick promoted science, he also signed an agreement with the aviators, allowing them use of the Sikorsky S-38 for sixty days. Thereafter they would return the aircraft to Chicago "in as good condition as they received it, ordinary wear and tear excepted; provided, however, that the AVIATORS shall not be liable for any damage to or loss of said airplane by accident" (a clause Gast and Cramer would ultimately be thankful for). The fliers granted exclusive rights to the Tribune to all interviews, stories, and news, and they agreed to refrain from publishing anything related to the flight until "after the newspaper publicity concerning the flight or attempted flight has ended." [88]

As the fliers awaited word from the Chicago weather bureau—whose predictions of favorable weather would decide when the S-38 could take off—only the aircraft's regular fuel tanks were filled, since the ship was less buoyant in the fresh water of Lake Michigan than it would be in the salt water of James Bay, where the auxiliary tanks would be filled. The weather bureau reported a nasty low pressure weather system stalled over Labrador, but a favorable ridge of high pressure crawling eastward from western Canada to supplant it. The meteorologists expected the ridge to produce good flying weather for the first two days of the projected five-day hop to Berlin.

"Today we fly to Berlin," wrote Wood in the Tribune of July 3, 1929. "Our course lies over strange lands where the drone of an airplane motor aloft is unknown." He continued,

Tossed on a pile of furs, skis, and Arctic equipment in the cabin of the 'Untin' Bowler . . . is a government mail bag. In it is a package of letters addressed in a dozen foreign languages to the Kings and Presidents of as many foreign kingdoms and republics. We hope to deliver that bag to the postmaster at Berlin before another week rolls around —the first air mail to be carried from Chicago to Europe. [89]

3 ON THAT MORNING of July 3, 1929, five thousand people crowded along the 8th Street beach to see the S-38 take off. At 8:30 a.m., Gast, Cramer, and Wood gave farewell hugs to their mothers and then climbed into the 'Untin' Bowler. Gast waved to the crowd and flashed a bright smile. Shorty Cramer smiled and pointed a finger skyward. Then, amid cheers that resounded from the crowd and the bellows of boat horns along the lakefront, Gast rolled the big flying boat down the ramp and into the lake.

Gast taxied the S-38 out into the lake, planed the hull, then lifted her free of the suction of the water at 8:50. Returning at an altitude of barely ten feet, he flew past the crowd. "Some in the crowd feared that he would not be able to clear the high bank and the Field Museum, toward which Gast had pointed," the Tribune reported. "But as he neared the obstacle the 'Untin' Bowler responded to a slight touch on the controls and climbed safely upward."

A minute later the big plane floated past the beach again, this time at a comfortable flying height, and the pilot made a graceful salute to the spectators by dipping to the right and left. The flight to Berlin, a pioneer effort toward finding a practical way to cross the Atlantic by air, and to eliminate the hazards that most transoceanic routes have had to conquer, was on. [90]

THE S-38 WINGED north at an altitude of 500 feet. The expedition stopped briefly at Milwaukee at 9:40 a.m., where the fliers made a quick pilgrimage to the statue of Leif Erikson, and at Sault Ste. Marie, where they arrived at 1:40 p.m. and spent an hour and a half clearing customs. The first day of flying ended at 7:40 p.m., EST, at Remi Lake in Canada, 660 miles from Chicago. The Canadian Provincial Air Service provided refueling there "as the big amphibion rocked in the crystal waves in a background of pine trees." [91] Cramer went to the radio and contacted Tribune Tower, while Gast decided that the low rain clouds to the north ruled out their continuing to the scheduled first night's stop at Rupert House on James Bay.

Cramer and Gast face the reporters, July 3, 1929. NATIONAL ARCHIVES

Cramer and Gast mug for the cameras, July 3, 1929. NATIONAL ARCHIVES

The crowd at Grant Park, Chicago, July 3, 1929. NATIONAL ARCHIVES

Before darkness fell, Gast flew the S-38 seven miles to another part of the lake where they loaded an additional cache of fuel. "When they finished, the stars were out and rather than risk the danger of night flying in a strange country, Gast taxied the *Bowler* all the way back. Foresters stood on the shore swinging lanterns to guide the dark shadow moving slowly back over the lake, its motor shuddering the quiet of the night." [92]

The weather turned for the worse.

A T 6 : 0 0 A . M . on July 4, 1929, the S-38 left Remi Lake and the last northern wire connection to Chicago, and headed into the trackless wastes of the sub-Arctic. Visibility was unlimited as they flew over flat, thickly wooded country. A low-pressure system sat just over Port Burwell, while another moved east from Minnesota. Cramer's radio reports to Tribune Tower grew more fragmentary throughout the day. At 8:05, the S-38 was over Rupert House, a small settlement of 20 or 30 buildings on the Rupert River on James Bay. The flying boat docked off a sloping beach

alongside an old shipwreck. There they refueled and were off for Great Whale, farther north along the shore of Hudson Bay.

During the afternoon, short-wave stations at Elgin, Illinois, and at Port Burwell, showed that the *Bowler* had taken off from Rupert House and almost immediately ran into rain and poor visibility. "Landing 9:50 Great Whale. Weather bad," [93] read one of Cramer's few messages during the day. The *Tribune* reported:

Because of the advantage of distance and lack of interference by other stations, the Port Burwell station had much better reception of the message than at Elgin, where it was said that the listener, who had been on the set since 3 a.m., caught the first whir of the motor at 8:10 and that this continued weakly until the fade-out, which meant that the *Bowler* was sliding down to a landing.

On the other hand, the Canadian Marine station on Cape Chidley asserted that the signals were loud. Another station at Hope's Advance, across Ungava Bay from Port Burwell, also had good reception. [94]

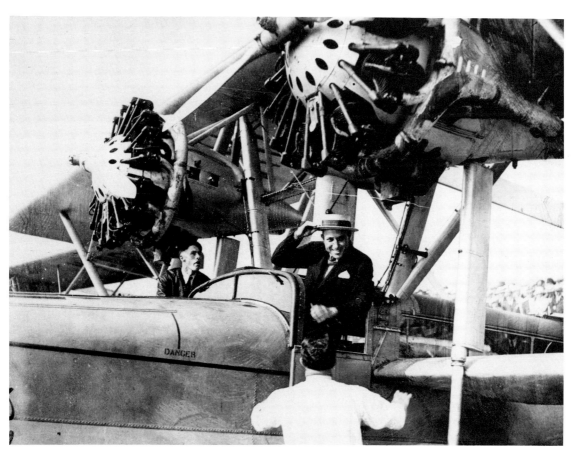

With a tip of his straw hat, Gast bids Chicago good-by, July 3, 1929. NATIONAL ARCHIVES

Lift-off from Grant Park, Chicago, July 3, 1929. NATIONAL ARCHIVES

In fact, fog had forced the S-38 back to Rupert House, where the ship once again tied up alongside the riverboat shipwreck. After taking on more fuel, the S-38 took off again toward Great Whale. Caches of fuel—"all of it pretty old"[95]—were found en route at Eastmain and Port George. At Port George, it took from four in the afternoon until midnight to siphon a few gallons of fuel into the S-38s tanks; no pumps were available there. Before six the next morning, before the tide went out, the flying boat was in the air again, flying over "green swamp and moss and hills covered with rock outcropping."[96] Then, with fog again closing in, Gast decided not to risk a flight to Port Burwell. He picked up the Great Whale River fifty miles inland and followed it to the Hudson Bay

Company's trading post at the mouth of the river on Hudson Bay.

Colonel McCormick, when he was able finally to reach the flyers by radio, reiterated his strict orders that the expedition was to use the weather to its advantage and take no unnecessary risks. Gast was ready to attempt the 600-mile hop to Port Burwell, but the weather reported there—32 degrees and foggy—held him fast.

Throughout July 5 and 6, the weather pinned the S-38 at the settlement of Great Whale. On July 7, the day they were to have arrived in Berlin, Gast, even with continuing overcast, risked the flight to Port Burwell.

ONE ANGLE OF THE BOWLER'S FLIGHT

"One Angle of the *Bowler*'s Flight," by McCutcheon, *Chicago Tribune*, July 5, 1929. Courtesy of *Chicago Tribune*

-52-

Cramer leads the welcoming committee in Milwaukee, July 3, 1929. NATIONAL ARCHIVES

At the Canadian border, July 3, 1929. NATIONAL ARCHIVES

Into Canada, NATIONAL ARCHIVES

The *'Untin' Bowler* over Remi Lake. NATIONAL ARCHIVES

Moored at Remi Lake. NATIONAL ARCHIVES

Robert Gast, Robert Wood, and Parker D. "Shorty" Cramer, in front of the S-38 *'Untin' Bowler*, at Remi Lake, Ontario, Canada, during the July 1929 expedition. NATIONAL ARCHIVES

"A few gallons of gasoline and a little oil doesn't make a base. . . ." National Archives

With help from native Canadians, the S-38 is refueled. National Archives

Refueling with Mobiloil Aero "H." NATIONAL ARCHIVES

4 DURING FLIGHT, the hum from the generators attached to the engines of the S-38 could be heard by radio stations from hundreds of miles away. On July 7, 1929, the radio station as Elgin reported picking up the amphibian's signals for five and a half hours. On July 8, the station at Port Burwell reported hearing the S-38 between 10:30 and 10:40 a.m. only. Other stations were similarly disappointed. The Sikorsky flying boat seemed to be lost amid the vast low plain of Ungava, the most desolate of Canadian wilds.

"It is a veritable 'no man's land' of muskeg swamps, rock, and stunted forests. . . ." the *Tribune* lamented. "Of government patrols in this territory there are none — no fire rangers and no forest fire protective planes, for it is all beyond the limit of marketable timber growth, and stunted birch, balsam fir, black and white spruce, and larch, dot the landscape." [97]

"They'll never make it at this time of year," warned Squadron Leader T.A. Lawrence of the Royal Canadian Air Force, when interviewed by the Ottawa *Journal*. "The best thing they can do, while they still have time, is to turn right around and go home. They should have waited until the water of the north coun-

try was all open and their amphibion of some real use in that territory. Or they should have taken off weeks earlier — about the beginning of June, when winter still held the Hudson Bay district in its grasp and there would have been natural landing fields everywhere on land and sea."

As to the possibility that the flyers might be down and lost in Ungava, Squadron leader Lawrence said: "God help them if they land there. . . . [They] might as well be in the north of Greenland or at the pole itself, for all the assistance and promise nature has to offer them there." [98]

FOUR HOURS AFTER leaving Hudson Bay at Great Whale, the S-38 sailed over Ungava Bay, crossed a field of icebergs, and headed toward Port Burwell along the jagged eastern coast of the bay. Following the twisted shoreline, Gast flew the S-38 to within forty miles of Port Burwell before a looming front forced him to turn the ship around and flee toward the Hudson Bay Company's post at Fort Chimo, on the Koksoak-River. A short conference with Cramer and Wood decided that the weather wasn't bad enough to lose the 100 miles back to Fort Chimo, so Gast instead brought the S-38 down to 300 feet, where they sighted an island. They made for a narrow channel near the island where the bigger ice was barred from entering and where the flying boat found an ice-free landing area. The three waited there for the dark, chill skies to clear.

"That was Sunday afternoon," wrote Wood. "There was no sleep that night or the night following."

Great chunks of melting snow broke from the crevices of the rocks and plunged into the water. At first we thought it was the distant rumble of thunder.

. . . three Eskimos hunting seals on the northern shore of the bay sighted the *Bowler* riding at anchor and scrambled through the ice in their kayaks, defying all laws of equilibrium. The three brown men, with walrus-like mustaches, came and stood thunderstruck before the big kayak with the wings. There ensued a conversation in which Shorty Cramer employed a half-dozen Eskimo words to learn the direction and distance from Port Burwell, on Cape Chidley.

"Kidley ugh," the trio replied, motioning to the northwest. Cramer wrote a message to the Northwest Mounted Police at Port Burwell, stating that we were down, waiting for the fog to clear, 40 miles south of Port Burwell, that the plane and crew were safe, but might be marooned for several days, and if possible to reach us by motor boat. [99]

With a fine ignorance of the value of money in the Arctic, the stranded crew "gave the Eskimos the note and a twenty-dollar bill."[100] They were helpless. Even their radio had to remain silent. In order to use it, the left engine had to be run up to charge the batteries, but the engine could not be cut on for fear that it would pull the ship onto the rocks.

On Monday morning the fog lifted, and Gast took off as soon as it did. A half hour later the fog rolled in again, and again the ship was forced into ice-strewn Ungava Bay. The *Tribune* later reported:

All day and into the night the fog hung over the island, covering the mainland a half mile away. . . . At the first sign of daylight, the fog lifted again. We weighed anchor and were in the air again before 2 o'clock. Fog lay in about the hills as the *Bowler* flew northward. We caught the first sight of the lofty Labrador mountains to the east. Cape Chidley and the whole northern point of Labrador was blanketed in fog with only the tops of the mountains visible. "Not a chance in the world of finding Burwell in that mess," Gast shouted back into the cabin.

We landed in a fjord a moment later. The fog bore down again. This was to be the last of the worst fog on the records of the meteorological station at Port Burwell.

At 4 o'clock a warm sun climbed into the bay and a northwest wind started the fog southward.

At 5:50 o'clock the operators of the Canadian Government radio station, who have awaited the *Bowler* since Thursday, heard the drone of the Sikorsky motors in the clouds. It was not until twenty minutes later that Gast and Cramer sighted the three houses which comprise the settlement, hidden in the tumbling hills of Cape Chidley.[101]

After this extraordinary battle with the ice and fog of Ungava Bay, the flying boat touched down in ice-strewn Amittoq Inlet near Port Burwell at 7:10 a.m. on July 9, 1929, six days out from Chicago and still a long way from Berlin.

Moored in a small cove, Amittoq Inlet, Port Burwell, July 10, 1929. NATIONAL ARCHIVES

5 WEATHER AND ICE trapped the flying boat in Amittoq Inlet, a long, narrow, river-like cut with 30-foot tides. The crew gathered all of the tiny community of Port Burwell to help them save the ship from the murderous ice. The natives stood regular watches around the ship, wielding long poles to fend off encroaching ice. Several times on July 10, the S-38 was nearly smashed on the rocks of the inlet. Even if the shifting ice had not held the ship in the inlet, bad weather made the next hop to Greenland impossible. Rain and poor visibility stretched from Port Burwell north along the coast of Baffin Land and across Davis Straight.

"All day long," wrote Wood, "an endless line of Eskimos swung across the mountain, which stands between the harbor, where the fuel is stored, and the fjord, where the *Bowler* is anchored. Each native bore ten gallons of gasoline on his back. It was a rough, hard climb up a steep cliff, over the jagged mountain and up and down another precipice to the shore, but the little brown men went about their task cheerily. Chesley Ford, factor of the Hudson Bay post here, will give them each a portion of tobacco for their trouble and they will be well satisfied."[102] Wood understated the wages, for the "little brown men" also received $4 per day and $5 per night for their labor.

This ad hoc refueling operation was interrupted several times when drifting ice threatened the ship, and when the tidal rush was ready to leave the flying boat high and dry on the rocks. That night the icepack created a small natural harbor around the S-38, and thereby saved the ship from being swept to sea by the tidal outflow. At midnight, as the inlet waters receded, Gast taxied the plane into the stream and moored it there. The Eskimos had loaded over two tons of fuel into the ship. All tanks, including the transatlantic auxiliaries, were topped off. The expedition's crew could now only fend off the ice and hope for a break in the weather.

Note from Robert Wood to Parker Cramer, written at Amittoq Inlet, July, 1929. It reads: "Shorty— the other pontoon has been torn almost loose. It's in bad shape. Better come down & take a look at it. Wood."
COURTESY OF THE WILLIAM H. CRAMER COLLECTION

IN THE MORNING, on July 11, 1929, an ice jam formed in the inlet, pushing the S-38 onto rocks and punching a small hole three feet above the waterline. Gast and Cramer repaired the damage, while six Eskimos sat on the wings and tail, pushing away chunks of ice with long poles. After noon, the tide fell back, and left the flying boat stranded on the rocks.

THE NEXT DAY, a chunk of ice as big as a house drifted into Amittoq Inlet and nearly crushed the S-38. Part of one rudder was crumpled, but Gast and Cramer, using the small machine shop at Port Burwell, repaired the damage. At each low tide, the S-38 settled onto bare rocks in the small cove. The duralumin hull took a beating. For the first time, Wood began to doubt they would ever leave Port Burwell on the flying boat. He wrote for the *Tribune*:

> A large plane is . . . unsuited for flying in this country. Save for a few plateaus south of Ungava Bay, we found no landing spaces along the whole route from Sault Ste. Marie. On the plateaus a landing could likely be made without casualty, but a crack-up would be almost certain. On the other hand, there is an abundance of water, excepting for a stretch of 150 miles between Remi Lake and Hanna Bay.
>
> The *Bowler* was never out of gliding distance of a good-sized body of water, and we have not once used the wheels for a landing. . . . Along Hudson Bay from Fort George to Great Whale, and from there to Ungava Bay fifteen or twenty lakes could be seen from the *Bowler* at almost any point along the route. Because this region is unexplored the lakes do not show on the map.[103]

WHEN THE ICE briefly moved from Amittoq Inlet into Ungava Bay on Saturday morning, July 14, Gast started the engines and taxied the S-38 out of inlet, around a point, and into Fox Harbor, closer to the settlement at Port Burwell. During the day, with the flying boat resting partly over the ice and partly over open water, Gast and Cramer had both slipped and fallen into the icy water, saving themselves at the last moment by grasping one of the many struts of the S-38.

The flying boat was moored there to a seemingly stable plate of ice at the head of the harbor, a few hundred yards from the abandoned Moravian Church. The crew was now ready to leave Labrador for Greenland as soon as the sky cleared and a few rudder fittings were mended. At 8:00 that night, after the S-38 was moored, the crew returned to the machine shop, located in a small hangar used for Canadian government aircraft in their first aerial explorations of Ungava Bay. There the broken rudder fittings were under repair. Gast and Cramer warmed themselves.

The barometer dropped and the wind rose. Disaster came gradually that evening.

Natives look on as ice threatens the S-38 at Port Burwell. NATIONAL ARCHIVES

At 9:30 an Eskimo came running over the hills. He had been sent by Corporal McInnes of the Mounted Police, who had been watching the plane, to tell us that the winds had cracked the solid ice. When we arrived at the point where the *Bowler* had been anchored, the ship was already in midstream and on its way to open water. [104]

Twenty times the crew of the flying boat and the small Arctic community at Port Burwell fended off the encroaching ice. Their efforts were not enough.

6 MCCORMICK'S magnificent Sikorsky S-38 seaplane, a shiny new example of the most prolific aircraft of its day, sank amid ice floes that night, in the middle of July. Wood described the disaster.

Its nose was in the air and its tail half submerged. A huge chunk of ice had broken from the middle of the stream and was drifting swiftly before the wind with the *Bowler* lashed to the forward edge. Had Corporal McInnes and the natives been on

the ice at the time it broke away, they would have been blown to sea with the ship. A half dozen persons had been on the ice all day, working on the plane.

The force of the ice had pushed the hull of the ship upward and the tail downward. One wing settled into the water. Water filled the cabin and the tail sank slowly, although it was not until the *Bowler* had floated two miles out into the sea that it disappeared. Air compartments in the hull and the hollow wings gave it buoyancy.

Gast, Parker Cramer and the little colony that has fought with us to save the *Bowler* from destruction, climbed up the rocks to a high promontory overlooking Hudson Straits, and there watched the plane drift toward a gray horizon and finally slip into the sea. It was a disheartening spectacle. Gast was deeply moved. . . .

The *Bowler* went to its grave with both pontoons lashed to the lower wings with rope. A ring strut was snapped in two. The fabric had been ripped from the lower wing. Big rents were torn in the tail surfaces; water filled the hull where it had poured through the hole, and the bracing wires and struts of the plane were pinched. While it would have required several days, the pilots believed it was possible to repair the ship. All the damage was caused by the buffeting of the tide and the battering of the ice.

At the time the ice broke, we were finishing the repair of fittings for the pontoons in the hope of fastening them on early in the morning. With these repaired, Gast planned to attempt to take off at low tide and fly a mile further inland to Mission, where a small protected body of water offered a possible landing place. A landing there would have been a gamble, but it would have been possible to beach the ship and proceed with repairs. We would have been unable to take off, however, for at least ten days until the ice broke from the end of the cove.

When we returned from watching the *Bowler* sinking, Mission Cove was entirely clear of ice. . . .

With his two companions, Shorty Cramer was stranded at the scene of its demise—a grey and lonely place called Port Burwell, an outpost "on the Labrador," in the ancient phrase of the schoonermen, where the bitter elements eventually forced away even the durable Hudson Bay Company. Though he never showed it, Cramer must have been despondent. His second attempt in two years to pioneer a northern air route from America to the Old World had ended in failure, even though he himself had survived to fly again.

In part, Cramer blamed himself. "We 'muffed' one thing: While we had cached supplies along the route, this cannot be construed as establishing a base ex-cept in the crudest sense of the word. We had made no provisions for handling such large equipment as the Sikorsky and it was due to this omission that we lost the plane. . . . Because of the great range of the tide [at Port Burwell], rocky shores, and without ramps or barges upon which to beach the plane, the best we could do was to fend off the bergs while attempting to fuel." [105]

Not until the end of July were Gast, Cramer, and Wood able to board a ship at Port Burwell and begin their journey back to civilization. In the meantime, they lived and cavorted with the natives. On one occasion, Gast replaced the old bell on the abandoned Moravian church and rang it. Hearing the sound of religion for the first time in a decade, the Eskimos responded by gathering at the church in expectation of a sermon.

On July 28, 1929, a message arrived at Port Burwell. It was the note the crew had given to Eskimos twenty days earlier when the S-38 was forced down, forty miles to the south. Wood described the arrival: "The messengers came across the Port Burwell Harbor, leaping from one cake of ice to another and pushing before them a decrepit sail boat laden with half a dozen seals and three kayaks. They dropped anchor in Mission Cove, pushed their kayaks over board and paddled ashore." [106]

Native oars and sails had, for the moment, at least, outpaced the world's most advanced flying boat.

After the sinking, Gast poses in front of the kind of ice that wrecked the *'Untin' Bowler*, late July, 1929.

Gast with the residents of Port Burwell, late July, 1929.

Destiny and Seaplanes

There is a destiny about places. For each man there is a piece of territory that calls

to him, that appeals to something deep inside him.

HAMMOND INNES, *Campbell's Kingdom*, 1952

R O B E R T M c C O R M I C K , who thought that "the world deteriorated the farther one traveled from Chicago," [107] received in stride the news that his beautiful flying boat was wrecked at the forsaken outpost of Port Burwell. It was, all things considered, exciting copy, and sold newspapers. The Colonel quickly replaced his first S-38 with a second. He continued his aeronautical adventures into the 1950s.

After the failed Chicago-to-Berlin expedition, the crew of the *'Untin' Bowler* went their separate ways. McCormick's aviation editor survived until the 1960s. His hand-picked pilots, however, like his famous midwestern Republican isolationism, did not survive the 1930s.

R O B E R T W O O D , the amiable aviation editor, passed away in the 1960s after a long career as a *Tribune* correspondent. His wife apparently discovered all his memorabilia of the S-38 expedition and donated the lot to the National Archives.

O N A P R I L 1 0 , 1934, flying another S-38, in China—from Shanghai to Canton—Robert Gast flew into yet another bank of fog. This time he did not escape. Mail bags and debris found floating in Hangchow Bay the next day pinpointed the crash. Not until August 18 of that year was the body of Gast himself washed ashore and positively identified.

S H O R T Y C R A M E R continued to press his case for a Northern Air Route. He believed that the flight of the S-38 proved "that seaplane equipment was adaptable for this route . . . and the fact that we made numerous landings through Northern Canada proved, that so far the route was practicable. We discovered too, that a few cans of gasoline and a little oil do not constitute a base. It is just as important that means

for beaching the plane be provided as well." [108]

Little more than a month after his return from Port Burwell, Cramer shipped out to Antarctica as the chief pilot for Sir Hubert Wilkins on the Second Wilkins-Hearst Antarctic Expedition. A year earlier Wilkins had made the first airplane flights over the Antarctic continent.

Cramer returned to embark on a lecture tour arranged by his brother. Meanwhile, the Cramer brothers tried everything they could to obtain another seaplane for another assault on the Northern Route. But times and conditions had changed. The stock market had crashed while Shorty was on his way to the southern continent. When he returned six months later, he found companies unwilling to risk their money on a gamble that had already produced two failures. The Cramer brothers engineered a blizzard of letters to prospective sponsors, and each letter returned with the same bland pronouncements about economics.

Shorty Cramer felt other pressures as well. He had invested his life in the quest for a Northern Air Route, and now several well-heeled rivals were poised to launch northern expeditions of their own. Gino Watkins' British effort would soon land a ski-equipped plane at Angmagsallik on Greenland's eastern shore to attempt the still-unachieved first hop over the ice cap. Harvard University's Alexander Forbes set sail aboard the schooner *Ramah* in 1931, with two seaplanes aboard, to chart the coast of northern Labrador, the very kind of geographic legwork Cramer knew was essential to the northern route's success.

And Cramer's midwestern rival, Charles Lindbergh himself, was planning a seaplane expedition over the northern route. As a friend wrote to Cramer: "It seems almost needless to call your attention to the danger confronting your air route should Lindbergh anticipate your efforts. . . . If he should make his proposed northeastern flight he would rob you of certainly much of your earned credit. . . ." [109]

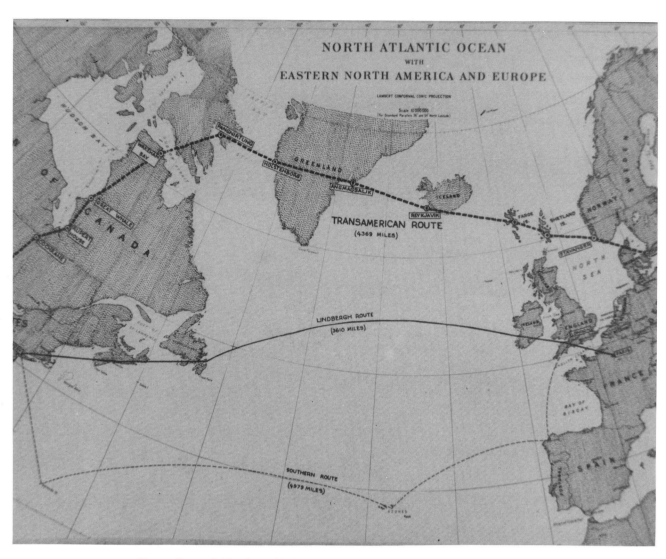

Shorty Cramer's Northern Air Route. Courtesy of the William H. Cramer Collection

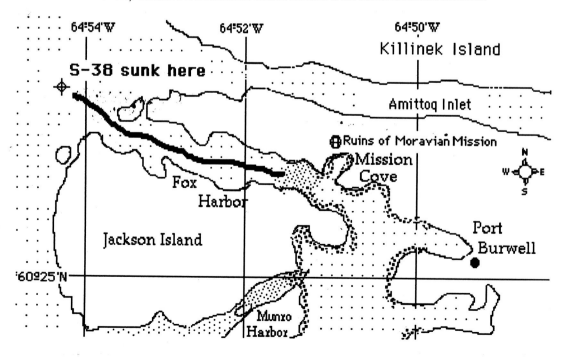

Port Burwell, northernmost Labrador, where the *'Untin' Bowler* sank in July, 1929. Flying Boat Society

Shorty Cramer with the
other members of the
Wilkins-Hearst Antarctic
Expedition, 1929–1930.
COURTESY OF THE
WILLIAM H. CRAMER COLLECTION

Oliver Pacquette and
Shorty Cramer before the
start of the August, 1931,
Northern Air Route flight.
COURTESY OF THE
WILLIAM H. CRAMER COLLECTION

Triumph! "Survey Plane
No. 1" at Angmagsallik,
after the first west-to-east
crossing of the Greenland
ice cap, August 7, 1931.
COURTESY OF THE
WILLIAM H. CRAMER COLLECTION

By June of 1931, Cramer accepted an offer from Transamerica Airlines, a small midwestern feeder line, to pilot their "Survey Plane No. 1," a small Bellanca seaplane, across the Northern Route. He lifted off in early August 1931, with a Canadian radio operator, Oliver Pacquette, and accomplished what no pilot had done before: the first west-to-east crossing of the Greenland Ice Cap. He continued on from Angmagsallik to Reykjavik, then to the Faroes and then the Shetland Islands. There, breathless, he had but one final short 200-mile hop to the coast of Norway, then on to Copenhagen and glory.

What happened next will probably never be known with certainty, but a careful examination of his brother's papers offers a plausible, if unsettling, explanation. The seaplane left Lerwick in the Shetland Islands, at 10:10 a.m., on Sunday morning, August 9. At 12:30, Paquette radioed that they had sighted the Norwegian coast and were fighting a heavy storm, but they expected to arrive in Copenhagen at 4:30. The two were never identifiably heard from again, though scattered, unverified and faint radio transmissions from the plane were reported as late as the next day, along with reports that the seaplane was sighted flying over the Orkney island of Westray, far to the west of the coast of Norway.

Two days after their takeoff from Lerwick, on August 11, a lone man standing at Taftsness, the northernmost point on the island of Sanday in the Orkney Islands, watched in startled surprise as a strong tide gently bore a seaplane shorewards. When the empty craft, in apparently good condition, was about 40 yards from shore, it was hit by a strong east-running current and carried out to sea again. [110]

Over a month would elapse before the wreckage of the Bellanca seaplane was located, about 300 miles southeast of Sanday. Assuming that the Sanday sighting is true, it is my hypothesis that, fogged in and unable to land along the treacherous Norwegian coast, Cramer attempted to regain Lerwick, but the storm's strong north winds pushed him south, towards the Orkneys. There, lost amid the tangle of islands, Cramer landed for the night. Taking off the next day, he would soon have run out of fuel, leaving the seaplane at the mercy of currents. Unable to moor or beach the plane, it is possible that Cramer and Pacquette made a swim for it as the floating aircraft neared one of the small islands, but did not survive the icy waters. Their plane was then left to float like a ghost ship until, on September 17, 1931, it was finally recovered and brought to rest.

Wreckage of "Survey Plane No. 1," discovered in the North Sea, September 17, 1931. COURTESY OF THE WILLIAM H. CRAMER COLLECTION

HISTORY SOON rendered the Sikorsky S-38 flying boat a ghost ship itself. Yet, despite its occasional calamities, in the hands of skilled pilots (and with the servicing of a competent ground crew), the S-38 performed beyond what even Igor Sikorsky had hoped for based on his earlier S-34 and S-36 designs. By 1930, as Shorty Cramer sought financiers for his Northern Air Route, sophisticated preparations were underway to combine the S-38 with giant floating "seadromes," to create, in nine hops, the first transatlantic passenger service.

Each seadrome was to comprise a landing field with a hangar, hotel, meteorological towers and radio rooms. The first of a series of eight seadromes, 1,100 feet long by 300 feet wide and weighing 29,000 tons, was to have been anchored by a 17,900-foot wire cable to the high flats of the ocean floor 350 miles off Sandy Hook, New Jersey. This first seadrome would have allowed the S-38 to provide the first regular aerial passenger and mail service between New York and Bermuda. The high cost of the project—each seadrome would have cost nearly two million dollars—combined with an absence of interest on the part of the U.S. government, conspired to keep the project in the imagination of its designer, former chief engineer of the Dupont Corporation, Edward R. Armstrong.[111]

The S-38 would never become the transatlantic airliner Shorty Cramer envisioned. His dream of a Northern Air Route did become reality—ten years after his disappearance. As a dictator ruled in Berlin and his Nazi hordes in 1939 marched across Europe, England fought to save itself. The U.S. had not yet entered the war, yet President Franklin D. Roosevelt in early 1941 ordered that a series of Northern Air Route bases be established so that short-range fighters could fly directly to the aid of Churchill and the British. The Northern Air Route provided an alternative to freighters crossing the ocean and the attendant risk of being torpedoed by German U-boats.

ALTHOUGH THE S-38 did not become the first transatlantic airliner, it was the first of Igor Sikorsky's aircraft to carry the Sikorsky name around the world. And following his credo that a machine was only as good as its designer, Sikorsky himself occasionally took a turn at the helm. He, for example, piloted one of his S-38s from Connecticut to Mexico, halfway to its delivery destination in Chile, in January 1931. His description of the flight is yet another example of the S-38's versatility when operating in an extraordinarily wide environmental spectrum.

. . . we took off from the ground from the Bridgeport Airport, since the water was covered with floating ice. A few hours later we arrived in Miami, and the next morning landed in warm, tropical Havana, where we went for a swim. This ship had no radio on board, and therefore, we preferred to continue the flight from Havana over the open sea and over inaccessible parts of Central America, following closely a regular Pan American Airways southbound airliner. This ship was another S-38, which was very pleasing to me. During the flight I spent most of my time behind the controls of this excellent, maneuverable airplane. It was interesting to fly over unknown country above the clouds and around the mountains and volcanoes of Central America. During this part of the trip we needed no navigation, because we simply trailed the other S-38 that was flying ahead of us.[112]

Igor Sikorsky followed the success of his S-38 even with the greater achievements of his larger four-engined transoceanic flying boats (ships that would need no seadrome to hop the Atlantic). In terms of production, however, the S-38 won all prizes. Sikorsky produced more S-38 amphibians than the total of all his other flying boats combined. The S-38 created Sikorsky Aircraft as a legitimate aircraft manufacturing company. The S-38 prompted the company's relocation from Long Island to the banks of the Housatonic River in Connecticut. It earned for Igor Sikorsky the recognition—and with it the financing—of the United Aircraft & Transport Corporation.

As the air yacht of explorers, the S-38 surveyed and opened the first air routes along the chain of the Leeward and Windward Islands of the Caribbean Sea and on into Central and South America, as well as throughout the Hawaiian Islands. And it carried dreamers to the end of their dreams.

In the end, one by one, the 101 amphibians were discarded. They rotted in Central American jungles, crashed into isolated mountainsides, were scrapped after valiant service, or sunk in some of the world's most isolated seas—but only because the S-38 was the only aircraft of its time that could reach such remote sites. Not a single specimen survives in museums, in aviation collections, or in private hands today.

The S-38 'Untin' Bowler, sunk by high winds and currents off Fox Harbor, likely rests on the bottom not far from where Gast, Cramer, Wood, and the people of the tiny settlement of Port Burwell watched it go down. The low salinity, 29° water temperature, and absence of wood borers—all factors that combine, in reverse, to destroy similar artifacts in the tropics—at that high latitude have likely kept it well preserved these last seven decades. If an S-38 still exists, that chance is by far the greatest at the bottom of Ungava Bay near Fox Harbor, northernmost Labrador. If found, it would be an artifact with a remarkable memory.

The Sikorsky S-40. UTC ARCHIVE   The Sikorsky S-42. UTC ARCHIVE

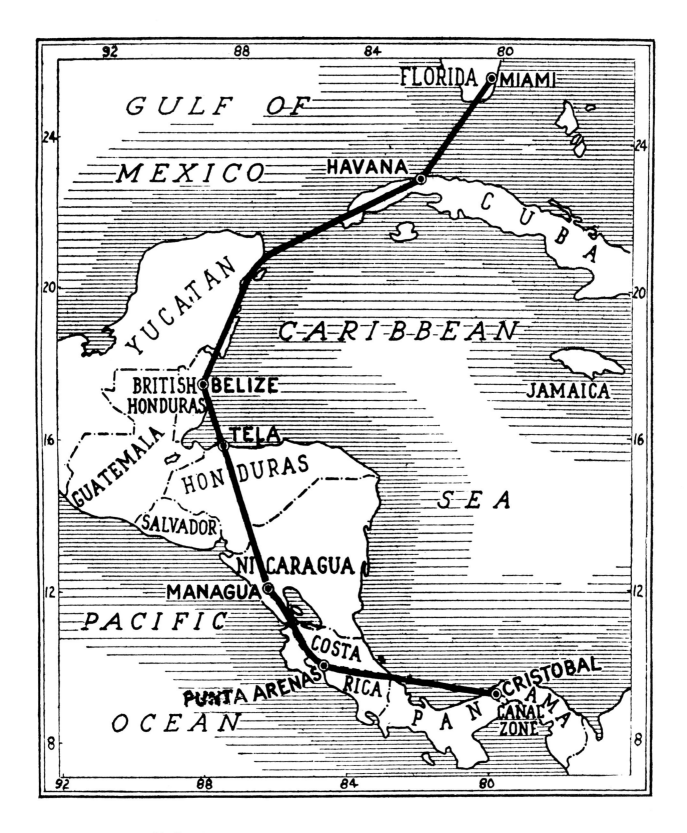

Lindbergh's route from Miami to Panama, February, 1929. UTC ARCHIVES

Appendix One

SIKORSKY S-38 AMPHIBIAN FLYING BOAT
Weight, Useful Load, and Performance*

WEIGHT
Gross Weight	10,480 lbs.
Weight Empty	6,460 lbs. (Amphibian)
Weight Empty	5,924 lbs. (Flying Boat)

USEFUL LOAD
Useful Load	4,020 lbs. (Amphibian)
Useful Load	4,556 lbs. (Flying Boat)

PERFORMANCE

	Amphibian		Flying Boat	
	425 hp Engine	575 hp Engine	425 hp Engine	575 hp Engine
High Speed	127.5	143.6	129.5	149
Cruising Speed	110	124	113	125
Initial Climb	870	1,000	950	1,100
Ceiling (Service)	16,000	18,000	17,000	19,000

*from a letter from M.E. Gluhareff, Chief of Design, Sikorsky Aircraft, to E.P. Warner, Editor, Aviation Magazine, June 3, 1932, Sikorsky Aircraft Flying Boat Papers, United Technologies Corporation.

Appendix Two

SIKORSKY S-38 AMPHIBIAN FLYING BOAT
Civil Aeronautics Authority Approved Type Certificates (ATC)*

Type:	S-38A PCAmB (Passenger Carrying Amphibian)
ATC No.	60
Approved:	May, 1928
Engines:	Two (2) Pratt & Whitney Wasps
Power:	420 hp each
Fuel:	n/a
Oil:	n/a
No. Seats:	n/a
No. Passengers:	Nine
Baggage:	500 lbs.
Stand Weight:	10,480 lbs.

Type:	S-38AH PCAmB
ATC No.	2-36
Approved:	n/a
Engines:	Two (2) Pratt & Whitney Hornets
Power:	525 hp each
Fuel:	n/a
Oil:	n/a
No. Seats:	n/a
No. Passengers:	n/a
Baggage:	n/a
Stand Weight:	10,480 lbs.

Type:	S-38B 10 PCAmB or 10 PCFbB (Flying Boat)
ATC No.	126
Approved:	May, 1929
Engines:	Two (2) Pratt & Whitney Wasps
Power:	420 hp each
Fuel:	330 gal.
Oil:	34 gal.
No. Seats:	Ten
No. Passengers:	Eight
Baggage:	500 lbs.
Stand Weight:	10,480 lbs.; 9,980 as Flying Boat
Remarks:	Eligible as flying boat with landing gear removed. Weight of landing gear approximately 500 lbs.

Type:	S-38BH PCAmB
ATC No.	356
Approved:	n/a
Engines:	Two (2) Pratt & Whitney Hornets
Power:	575 hp each
Fuel:	n/a
Oil:	n/a
No. Seats:	n/a
No. Passengers:	Eight
Baggage:	710 lbs.
Stand Weight:	10,480 lbs.

Type:	S-38BS 7PCAmB
ATC No.	2-434
Approved:	n/a
Engines:	Two (2) Pratt & Whitney Wasps
Power:	450 hp each
Fuel:	330 gal.
Oil:	34 gal.
No. Seats:	Seven
No. Passengers:	Five
Baggage:	600 lbs.
Stand Weight:	10,480 lbs.

Type:	S-38BT PCAmB
ATC No.	2-446
Approved:	n/a
Engines:	Two (2) Pratt & Whitney Wasps
Power:	525 hp each
Fuel:	n/a
Oil:	n/a
No. Seats:	n/a
No. Passengers:	Eight
Baggage:	271 lbs.
Stand Weight:	10,480 lbs.

Type:	S-38 (Special) PCAmB
ATC No.	2-68
Approved:	n/a
Engines:	Two (2) Pratt & Whitney Wasps
Power:	420 hp each
Fuel:	n/a
Oil:	n/a
No. Seats:	n/a
No. Passengers:	Nine
Baggage:	400 lbs.
Stand Weight:	10,480 lbs.

Type:	S-38C

ATC No.	158
Approved:	June, 1929
Engines:	Two (2) Pratt & Whitney Wasps
Power:	420 hp each
Fuel:	330 gal.
Oil:	34 gal.
No. Seats:	12
No. Passengers:	Ten
Baggage:	400 lbs.
Stand Weight:	10,480 lbs.

From: Igor Alexis Sikorsky. The Technical History of Sikorsky Aircraft and its Predecessors (Since 1909) (Stratford, CT: Sikorsky Aircraft Corporation, May, 1966), Archive and Historical Resource Center, United Technologies Corporation, East Hartford, CT.

Appendix Three

SIKORSKY S-38 AMPHIBIAN FLYING BOAT
*International Air Records**

Altitude (C2 — Seaplanes)

Payload — 500 klgm.

Date:	July 21, 1930
Altitude:	26,929.08 ft.
Pilot:	Boris Sergievsky
Power:	Two Pratt & Whitney 575 hp Hornets
Place:	Bridgeport, Connecticut
Remarks:	Held until January 26, 1934; class discontinued after 1939.

Payload — 1000 klgm

Date:	July 21, 1930
Altitude:	26,929.08 ft.
Pilot:	Boris Sergievsky
Power:	Two Pratt & Whitney 575 hp Hornets
Place:	Bridgeport, Connecticut
Remarks:	Held until December 26, 1933.

Payload — 2000 klgm

Date:	August 11, 1930
Altitude:	19,709.25 ft.
Pilot:	Boris Sergievsky
Power:	Two Pratt & Whitney 575 hp Hornets
Place:	North Beach, Long Island, New York
Remarks:	Held until January 3, 1934.

From: Igor Alexis Sikorsky. The Technical History of Sikorsky Aircraft and its Predecessors (Since 1909) (Stratford, CT: Sikorsky Aircraft Corporation, May, 1966), Archive and Historical Resource Center, United Technologies Corporation, East Hartford, CT.

Appendix Four

SIKORSKY S-38 AMPHIBIAN FLYING BOAT
*Production and Sales Summary**

No.	Mfg. No.	License No.	Customer
Prototype			
A	14-A	NC-5933	New York, Rio, Buenos Aires Lines (NYRBA)
Initial Production Run			
1	14-1	NC-8000	Pan American Airways
2	14-2	NC-8005	J.H. Whitney
3	14-3	NC-8019	Curtiss Flying Service
4	14-4	NC-8020	Pan American Airways
5	14-5	NC-8021	Western Air Express
6	14-6	NC-8022	Pan American Airways
7	14-7	NC-8043	John Hertz
8	14-8	NC-	U.S. Navy
9	14-9	NC-	U.S. Navy
10	14-10	NC-8044	Pan American Airways
Production Runs			
1	114-1	NC-9753	Col. R.R. McCormick
2	114-2	NC-9775	Pan American Airways
3	114-3	NC-9776	Pan American Airways
4	114-4	NC-9105	James C. Willson
5	114-5	NC-9106	Pan American Petroleum Corp.
6	114-6	NC-9107	Pan American Airways
7	114-7	NC-9143	Curtiss-Wright Flying Service
8	114-8	NC-9144	Curtiss-Wright Flying Service
9	114-9	NC-9137	Pan American Airways
10	114-10	NC-9151	Pan American Airways
11	114-11	NC-9138	Colonial Western Airways
12	114-12	A-8284	U.S. Navy
13	114-13	NC-9139	Sikorsky Aviation Corporation Demonstration Model #1 (Dismantled in 1932)
14	114-14	NC-9140	Andean National Corporation
15	114-15	A-8285	U.S. Navy
16	114-16	NC-196-H	Curtiss-Wright Flying Service
17	114-17	A-8287	U.S. Navy
18	114-18	NC-158-H	Colonial Western Airways
19	114-19	NC-159-H	Col. George R. Hutchinson
20	114-20	NC-160-H	C.R. Wahlgreen
21	214-1	NC-197-H	Pan American Airways
22	214-2	NC-198-H	Canadian Colonial Airways
23	214-3	NC-199-H	Southern Sugar Co.
24	214-4	NC-73-K	NYRBA
25	214-5	NC-74-K	John Hertz
26	214-6	NC-75-K	Pan American Airways
27	214-7	NC-111-M	Inter-Island Airways
28	214-8	NC-112-M	Inter-Island Airways
29	214-9	A-8286	U.S. Navy
30	214-10	NC-113-M	NYRBA
31	214-11	AC-29406	U.S. Army
32	214-12	NC-141-M	Public Service Co. of No. Illinois
33	214-13	NC-142-M	Pan American Airways
34	214-14	NC-143-M	J.M. Patterson**
35	214-15	NC-144-M	Pan American Airways
36	214-16	NC-145-M	Pan American Airways
37	214-17	NC-146-M	Pan American Airways
38	214-18	NC-300-N	Pan American Airways
39	214-19	NC-301-N	NYRBA
40	214-20	NC-302-N	NYRBA
41	314-1	NC-943-M	NYRBA
42	314-2	NC-94-M	NYRBA
43	314-3	NC-945-M	Pan American Airways

44	314-4	NC-946-M	NYRBA
45	314-5	NC-1-V	Col. R.R. McCormick
46	314-6	NC-2-V	Creole Petroleum Corporation
47	314-7	NC-3-V	Pan American Airways
48	314-8	NC-4-V	Inter-Island Airways
49	314-9	NC-5-V	United Aircraft Exports for China
50	314-10	NC-8-V	U.S. Navy
51	314-11	NC-7-V	American Airways, Inc.
52	314-12	NC-6-V	Pal-Waukee Airport†
53	314-13	NC-9-V	U.S. Navy
54	314-14	NC-10-V	American Airways, Inc.
55	314-15	NC-11-V	Margery Durant
56	314-16	NC-12-V	U.S. Navy
57	314-17	NC-13-V	U.S. Navy
58	314-18		Hull sold to U.S. Army
59	314-19	NC-15-V	United Aircraft Exports (for Capt. F. Francis, England)
60	314-20	NC-16-V	Pan American Airways (China)
61	414-1	NC-303-N	Grigsby-Grunow Co.
62	414-2	NC-304-N	Pan American Airways
63	414-3	NC-305-N	Inter-Island Airways
64	414-4	NC-306-N	Pan American Airways
65	414-5	NC-307-N	United Aircraft Exports for China
66	414-6	NC-308-N	NYRBA
67	414-7	NC-309-N	Pan American Airways
68	414-8	NC-17-V	Pan American Airways (China)
69	414-9	NC-18-V	Pan American Airways
70	414-10	NC-19-V	Pan American Airways
71	414-11	NC-20-V	United Aircraft Exports, Inc.
72	414-12	NC-21-V	Interstate Aeronautical Corp.
73	414-13	NC-22-V	Pan American Airways (Grace)
74	414-14	NC-23-V	Standard Oil Co.
75	414-15	NC-24-V	Howard Hughes
76	414-16	NC-25-V	Assigned for special tests
77	414-17	NC-26-V	United Aircraft Exports for Chile
78	414-18		U.S. Army
79	414-19	C.F.-ASO	Canadian Airways
80	414-20	NC-29-V	Martin Johnson
81	514-1		U.S. Army
82	514-2		U.S. Army
83	514-3		U.S. Army
84	514-4	NC-40-V	Pan American Airways
85	514-5		U.S. Army
86	514-6		U.S. Army
87	514-7		U.S. Army
88	514-8		U.S. Army
89	514-9		U.S. Army
90	514-10		U.S. Army

*From a document entitled "Sikorsky Aviation Corporation S-38," dated August 31, 1933, Sikorsky Aircraft Flying Boat Papers, United Technologies Corporation.
**214-14 delivered to Pratt & Whitney on October 1, 1929. Returned by them on March 23, 1931, in exchange for one S-39.
†314-12 delivered to the Cleveland Co., on June 30, 1930. Exchanged for an S-39 (#912) on July 25, 1932.

Appendix Five

SIKORSKY S-38 AMPHIBIAN FLYING BOAT
Last Known Whereabouts

No.	Mfg. No.	License No.	Last Reported Location
Prototype			
A	14-A	NC-5933	Scrapped by Pan Am, 7 October 1931, after sinking and salvage in Puerto Rico.*
Initial Production Run			
1	14-1	NC-8000	Registered to Pan Am, 1935.*
2	14-2	NC-8005	Registered to J. H. Whitney, 1928*
3	14-3	NC-8019	Lost at sea, February, 1929.‡
4	14-4	NC-8020	Scrapped by Pan Am, May, 1933.*
5	14-5	NC-8021	Wrecked during wheels down landing in Avalon Harbor, California, 5 June 1929.*
6	14-6	NC-8022	Registered to Curtiss-Wright Flying Service, October, 1930.*
7	14-7	NC-8043	Lost at sea while flying from Norfolk, Virginia, to Curtiss Field, New York, 23 March 1929. No trace recovered.*
8	14-8	NC-	Retired from U.S. Navy service, November, 1933.*
9	14-9	NC-	Retired from U.S. Navy service, November, 1933.*
10	14-10	NC-8044	Registered to Pan Am, 1935.*
Production Runs			
1	114-1	NC-9753	Sunk, Fox Harbor, Labrador, July 1929.
2	114-2	NC-9775	Registered to Embry-Riddle, Miami, Florida, in 1946–47.*
3	114-3	NC-9776	Registered to Embry-Riddle, Miami, Florida, in 1946.*
4	114-4	NC-9105	Registered to Despatch Corp., New York City, in 1935.*
5	114-5	NC-9106	Registered to Pan American Petroleum Corp., as of October, 1930.*
6	114-6	NC-9107	Crashed and destroyed while flying for Pan Am affiliate SCADTA in Colombia, South America, April, 1934.*
7	114-7	NC-9143	Registered to Curtiss-Wright Flying Service, as of January, 1932.*
8	114-8	NC-9144	Registered to Curtiss-Wright Flying Service, as of October, 1930.*
9	114-9	NC-9137	Registered to Pan Am, as of February, 1932.*
10	114-10	NC-9151	Owned by Bol-Inca Mining Corp., as of 1947.*
11	114-11	NC-9138	Owned by Bol-Inca Mining Corp., as of 1935.*
12	114-12	A-8284	Crashed, June, 1929, while flying for U.S. Navy.‡
13	114-13	NC-9139	Sikorsky Aviation Corporation. Used as Demonstrator No. 1, until dismantled in 1932.‡
14	114-14	NC-9140	Crashed June, 1929, while flying for Andean National Corporation.‡
15	114-15	A-8285	Operated by U.S. Navy, June, 1929.‡
16	114-16	NC-196-H	Crashed flying for Curtiss-Wright Flying Service, August, 1929.‡
17	114-17	A-8287	Operated by U.S. Navy, July, 1929.‡

18	114-18	NC-158-H	Upper wings recorded at the Charles H. Babb & Co., Glendale, California, in February, 1945, where permission was requested from Sikorsky to sell them to Expreso Aereo Inter-Americano, S.A., to repair 414-20, which had been damaged in a storm in Cuba.†
19	114-19	NC-159-H	Sunk south of Angmagssalik, Greenland, September, 1932.
20	114-20	NC-160-H	Operated in Kodiak, Alaska by W.J. Erskino, 1937.*
21	214-1	NC-197-H	Crashed and destroyed, Miami, Florida, 19 September 1929.*
22	214-2	NC-198-H	Operated by Colonial Air Transport, New York, in 1932.*
23	214-3	NC-199-H	Registered to George Daufkirch, Long Island, New York, in 1940.*
24	214-4	NC-73-K	Operated by Pan Am in Brazil in 1934.*
25	214-5	NC-74-K	Registered to Miami Seaplane Service in 1940-41.*
26	214-6	NC-75-K	Crashed and destroyed at Rio Branco, Brazil, in 1938, while flying for Panair of Brazil*
27	214-7	NC-111-M	Registered to Inter-Island Airways, Hawaii, in February, 1938.*
28	214-8	NC-112-M	Registered to Inter-Island Airways, Hawaii, in February, 1938.*
29	214-9	A-8286	Operated by U.S. Navy, September, 1929.‡
30	214-10	NC-113-M	Operated by NYRBA, September, 1929.‡
31	214-11	AC-29406	Operated by U.S. Army, January, 1930.‡
32	214-12	NC-141-M	Owned by Arthur L. Caperton, Glenview, Illinois, in 1931.*
33	214-13	NC-142-M	Sunk in landing accident on Kikori River, Australia, 27 December 1937.*
34	214-14	NC-143-M	Operated by Pan Am in 1934.*
35	214-15	NC-144-M	Operated by Pan Am in 1933.*
36	214-16	NC-145-M	Crashed and destroyed while flying for Panair of Brazil, July, 1933.*
37	214-17	NC-146-M	Registered to Pan Am as of 29 March 1943.*
38	214-18	NC-300-N	Operated by SCADTA, December, 1934.*
39	214-19	NC-301-N	Operated by SCADTA, late 1934.*
40	214-20	NC-302-N	Dismantled by Pan Am, December, 1930.*
41	314-1	NC-943-M	Registered to Colombian Petroleum Co., Inc., in 1937-38.*
42	314-2	NC-94-M	Crashed and destroyed flying for Pan Am, 14 June 1932.*
43	314-3	NC-945-M	Registered to Joseph P. Sheehan, Cambridge, Mass., in 1947.*
44	314-4	NC-946-M	Scrapped by Pan Am, August, 1933.*
45	314-5	NC-1-V	Damaged and never repaired following hurricane in Mazatlan, Mexico, in 1943.*
46	314-6	NC-2-V	Operated by Creole Petroleum Company in 1932.*
47	314-7	NC-3-V	Registered to Pan Am in August, 1934.*
48	314-8	NC-4-V	Registered to Hawaiian Airlines, 1947.*
49	314-9	NC-5-V	United Aircraft Exports for China, 1930
50	314-10	NC-8-V	Operated by U.S. Navy, 1930
51	314-11	NC 7 V	Registered to American Airlines, in 1936.
52	314-12	NC-6-V	While involved in aerial survey work in Indonesia, reported destroyed either during attack by Japanese Zero's on airport at Buitenzorg, Java, or soon after Japanese occupation in 1942.*
53	314-13	NC-9-V	Operated by U.S. Navy, 1930.
54	314-14	NC-10-V	Registered to American Airways in 1934.*
55	314-15	NC-11-V	Sold by Svensk Flygtjanst AB in Stockholm, Sweden, in 1936, to a French company in Africa.*
56	314-16	NC-12-V	Owned by U.S. Navy, 1930
57	314-17	NC-13-V	Owned by U. S. Navy, 1930.‡
58	314-18		Hull sold to U.S. Army, 1930.
59	314-19	NC-15-V	Owned by Compagnie des Chargeurs Reunis in Africa in 1939, where it was destroyed on 12 August at Calabar, Niger Colony.*
60	314-20	NC-16-V	Crashed and destroyed at Chusan Island, China, on 24 November 1933, while flying for Pan Am in China.*
61	414-1	NC-303-N	Registered to Bol-Inca Mining Corp., in 1935.*
62	414-2	NC-304-N	Registered to Pan Am in Brazil in 1938*
63	414-3	NC-305-N	Only Inter-Island Airways aircraft not damaged in Japanese attack on Pearl Harbor. Still registered to Inter-Island in 1946*
64	414-4	NC-306-N	Destroyed in a crash six miles south of France Field, Canal Zone, while flying for Pan Am on 7 February 1931.*
65	414-5	NC-307-N	United Aircraft Exports for China, apparently in 1933.*
66	414-6	NC-308-N	Scrapped by Pan Am 23 May 1934.*
67	414-7	NC-309-N	Crashed while operated by SCADTA in April, 1931.*
68	414-8	NC-17-V	Crashed into Hangchow Bay, China, on 10 April 1934, while operated by Chinese National Aviation Corp., pilot Robert Gast killed.
69	414-9	NC-18-V	Registered to Panagra, April, 1933.*
70	414-10	NC-19-V	Operated by Palm Beach Seaplane Service, Inc., West Palm Beach, Florida, in 1940.*
71	414-11	NC-20-V	Crashed and destroyed near Merida, Yucatan, Mexico, 9 September 1930.*
72	414-12	NC-21-V	Destroyed by fire in Biscayne Bay, Florida, 11 December 1941.*
73	414-13	NC-22-V	Registered to Panagra in 1939.*
74	414-14	NC-23-V	While involved in aerial survey work in Indonesia, reported destroyed either during attack by Japanese Zero's on airport at Buitenzorg, Java, or soon after Japanese occupation in 1942.*
75	414-15	NC-24-V	Owned by Howard Hughes, 1933.*
76	414-16	NC-25-V	Owned by Sikorsky Aircraft, destroyed by fire, 17 March 1930.‡
77	414-17	NC-26-V	United Aircraft Exports for Chile, 1932.
78	414-18		U.S. Army, 1933.§

79	414-19	C.F.-ASO	Registration cancelled by Canadian Airways, June, 1934.*
80	414-20	NC-29-V	Reported damaged by a windstorm in Cuba in February, 1945, while operating for Expreso Aereo Inter-Americano, S.A.†
81	514-1		U.S. Army, 1933.§
82	514-2		U.S. Army, 1933.§
83	514-3		U.S. Army, 1933.§
84	514-4	NC-40-V	Destroyed by storm at Hankow, China, 13 August 1935.*
85	514-5		U.S. Army, 1933.§
86	514-6		U.S. Army, 1933.§
87	514-7		U.S. Army, 1933.§
88	514-8		U.S. Army, 1933.§
89	514-9		U.S. Army, 1933.§
90	514-10		U.S. Army, 1933.§

*Mayborn, Mitch. "The Ugly Duckling: Sikorsky's S-38," *American Aviation Historical Society Journal*, Vol. 4, No. 3, Fall 1959.
**Mayborn, Mitch, "The Sikorsky S-38 in Australia and the Pacific," *American Aviation Historical Society Journal*, December, 1961.
†Letter from U.S. Aviation Underwriters Incorporated to Cance-Vought Aircraft, 19 February 1945, Sikorsky Flying Boat Records.
‡From a draft document entitled "Sikorsky Amphibian S-38," Sikorsky Flying Boat Records.
§Reported scrapped en masse after crash of Army S-38 (C-6A; 30-399) at Oceanside, California, that killed pilot and six passengers.

Aviation researchers with more detailed and/or precise information on the disposition of any of the 101 S-38s can correspond with the author in care of the following address:

Flying Boat Society
P. O. Box 1052
Abington, PA 19001

Notes, Part One

1. Richard C. Knott, *The American Flying Boat* (Annapolis, 1979), p. 212.
2. Igor I. Sikorsky, *The Story of the Winged-S* (New York, 1941), p. 186.
3. Knott, *American Flying Boat*, p. 118. See also: Edward Jablonski, *Seawings: The Romance of the Flying Boats* (Garden City, New York: Doubleday & Co., 1972), p. 31.
4. Mitch Mayborn, "The Ugly Duckling: Sikorsky's S-38," American Aviation Historical Society *Journal*, Vol. 4, No. 3, Fall 1959, p. 156.
5. Frederick H. Becker, " 'Hornets' on the Spanish Main," *The Bee-Hive*, March, 1929, Vol. III, No. 1, p. 11.
6. *Ibid.*, pp. 12–13.
7. Edward Jablonski, *Seawings: The Romance of the Flying Boats*, p. 52.
8. *Ibid.*, p. 53.
9. *Ibid.*, p. 54.
10. "Our Sikorsky is Delivered," *The Bee-Hive*, November, 1929, Vol. III, No. 9, p. 10.
11. Robert Wood, "From Aiken to Chicago: A Vignette of Modern Travel," *Liberty Magazine*, April 25, 1931, pp. 50–51.
12. Donald Dale Jackson, *The Explorers* (Chicago, 1983), p. 67.
13. Osa Johnson, *I Married Adventure* (Philadelphia, 1940), pp. 345–46.
14. Jablonski, *Seawings*, p. 71.
15. Johnson, *I Married Adventure*, p. 350.
16. *Ibid.*, p. 353.
17. *Ibid.*, p. 355.
18. *Ibid.*

19. "Sikorsky with Two Wasps Spends Year Surveying Venezuelan Wilderness," *The Bee-Hive*, May, 1931, Vol. V, No. 5, pp. 6–7.
20. *Ibid.*
21. *Ibid.*
22. H.F. Johnson, with Arthur Dailey. *Carnauba Expedition* (Racine, Wisconsin, 1936), pp. 4, 6.
23. *Ibid.*, p. 23.
24. *Ibid.*, p. 102.
25. *Ibid.*, p. 24.

Notes, Part Two

26. Frank J. Delear, *Igor Sikorsky: His Three Careers in Aviation* (New York: Dodd, Mead and Co., 1976), p. 109.
27. *Ibid.*, p. 124.
28. Igor I. Sikorsky, *The Story of the Winged-S* (New York, Dodd, Mead and Co., 1941), p. 178.
29. *Ibid.*, p. 180.
30. R.E.G. Davies, *Pan Am: An Airline and Its Aircraft* (New York, Orion Books, 1987), p. 28.
31. *The New York Times*, June 1, 1927, p. 2.
32. Richard C. Knott, *The American Flying Boat* (Annapolis, Naval Institute Press, 1979), p. 118.
33. Various numbers of S-36s have been credited. Knott (1979), Jablonski (1972), and a National Advisory Committee for Aeronautics (NACA) Aircraft Circular (1928) place the production at five, while Delear (1976) accounts for only two. The recent National Air & Space Museum (NASM) Sikorsky exhibit catalogue by Cochrane, Hardesty, and Lee (1989) places the number at six. Igor Sikorsky himself (1941), says only that: "A few ships of this type were sold, one of them to the United States Navy." Four are definitely established through photographic evidence and through their associations with other organizations or individuals. No internal Sikorsky documents for the S-36 survive.
34. Sikorsky Aviation Corporation, *Instructions for the Maintenance and Care of the Sikorsky Amphibion Type S-38* (Bridgeport, CT, n.d.), p. 14, National Air & Space Museum Archives.
35. Delear, *Igor Sikorsky*, p. 135.
36. Sikorsky Aviation Corporation, *Instructions for the Maintenance and Care of the Sikorsky Amphibion Type S-38* (Bridgeport, CT, n.d.), p. 24, National Air & Space Museum Archives.
37. *Ibid.*, p. 14.
38. *Ibid.*
39. *Ibid.*, p. 15.
40. National Advisory Committee for Aeronautics, *The Sikorsky Twin-Engined Amphibian Type S-38 Model 1928*, Aircraft Circular No. 79 (Washington, August, 1928), p. 5, National Air & Space Museum Archives.
41. Sikorsky Aviation Corporation, *Instructions for the Maintenance and Care of the Sikorsky Amphibion Type S-38* (Bridgeport, CT, n.d.), p. 24, National Air & Space Museum Archives.
42. *Ibid.*
43. Sikorsky Manufacturing Corporation, *Sikorsky Amphibion S-38* (College Point, Long Island, New York, 1928; prepared by Brearley Service of New York), p. 18, National Air & Space Museum Archives.
44. Sikorsky, *Winged-S*, p. 183.
45. *Ibid.*
46. Ralph B. Lightfoot, "Sikorsky Flying Boats," American Aviation Historical Society *Journal*, Vol. 24, No. 4, Winter 1979, p. 244.
47. *Sikorsky Aviation Corporation: S-38* (Sales Summary), August 31, 1933; and M.E. Gluhareff, Chief of Design, Sikorsky Aviation Corporation, to E.P. Warner, Editor, Aviation Magazine, June 3, 1932. Both formerly located in Sikorsky Aircraft Flying Boat Records, Archive and Historical Resource Center, United Technologies Corporation, East Hartford, CT.
These invaluable internal Sikorsky documents show that the U.S. Navy purchased ten S-38s, designating them XPS-2 and PS-3;

the U.S. Army purchased 12 S-38s, giving them the designation C-6.

The total number of S-38s built is generally recorded at 111, this figure being cited by every previous secondary account of Sikorsky history. This number is based on one prototype, plus Sikorsky's initial production run of ten, plus five production runs of 20 aircraft each, for a total of 111. These production runs of 20 were assigned numbers 114-1 through -20, 214-1 through -20, 314-1 through -20, 414-1 through -20, and 514-1 through -20. These internal Sikorsky documents, however, written after the last S-38 was built in January, 1931, show that production run 514 only reached from one to ten. Thus, the total number of S-38s built by Sikorsky was 101.

48. Manufacturer's Number 14-A, License Number NC-5933. NYRBA would eventually own and operate nine S-38s before the airline and its aircraft were absorbed by Pan American Airways on 15 September 1930. *Sikorsky Aviation Corporation: S-38* (Sales Summary), August 31, 1933, Sikorsky Aircraft Flying Boat Records, Archive and Historical Resource Center, United Technologies Corporation, East Hartford, CT.

49. Ralph A. O'Neill with Joseph F. Hood, *A Dream of Eagles* (San Francisco: San Francisco Book Co., 1973), pp. 127–128.

50. Manufacturer's Number 14-1, License Number NC-8000. *Sikorsky Aviation Corporation: S-38* (Sales Summary), August 31, 1933, Sikorsky Aircraft Flying Boat Records, Archive and Historical Resource Center, United Technologies Corporation, East Hartford, CT.

51. Sikorsky, *Winged-S*, p. 183.

52. *Ibid.*

53. *Ibid.*, p. 184.

54. *First Annual Report to Stockholders*, United Aircraft & Transport Corporation. (New York, 1930), p. 7.

55. Ralph B. Lightfoot, "Sikorsky Flying Boats," American Aviation Historical Society *Journal*, Vol. 24, No. 4, Winter 1979, p. 244.

56. *Sikorsky Amphibian S-38* (Sikorsky Aircraft Corporation draft document, n.d.), pp. 2–3, Sikorsky Aircraft Flying Boat Records, Archive and Historical Resource Center, United Technologies Corporation, East Hartford, CT.

57. *Ibid.*

58. *Sikorsky Amphibion S-38*, sales brochure, (Sikorsky Aircraft published document, n.d.), p. 4, Sikorsky Aircraft Flying Boat Records, Archive and Historical Resource Center, United Technologies Corporation, East Hartford, CT.

59. See Note 47.

60. National Advisory Committee for Aeronautics, *The Sikorsky Twin-Engined Amphibian Type S-38 Model 1928*, Aircraft Circular No. 79 (Washington, August, 1928), p. 3, National Air & Space Museum Archives.

61. *Test of the Sikorsky Amphibian S-38*, War Department, Air Corps Technical Report, Serial No. 3036 (Wright Field, Dayton, Ohio, March 18, 1929), p. 3a, National Air & Space Museum Archives.

62. *Ibid.*, pp. 1, 5.

63. Mitch Mayborn, "The Ugly Duckling: Sikorsky's S-38," American Aviation Historical Society *Journal*, Vol. 4, No. 3, Fall 1959, p. 156.

64. *Ibid.*, p. 159.

65. Robert Hanley, telephone conversation, September 26, 1988.

66. Mayborn, "The Ugly Duckling," pp. 160–161.

67. *Ibid.*, p. 160.

68. *Ibid.*, pp. 159–160.

69. Edward Jablonski, *Seawings: The Romance of the Flying Boats*, p. 65.

Notes, Part Three

70. Joseph Gies, *The Colonel of Chicago* (New York: E.P. Dutton, 1979), p. 101.

71. *Ibid.*

72. *Ibid.*, p. 119.

73. *Ibid.*

74. "[Parker Cramer] drove his [flying] machine under the Kittanning bridge. The present stage of water together with the width of the bridge between the [second and third] piers made the undertaking an unusually precarious one. [Said Cramer:] 'Every time I walked across the bridge I got the idea that I could drive my plane under it, and I couldn't get away from the idea. So I concluded to try it and say I am surely tickled I got away with it. . . . At the time the plane passed under the bridge it was travelling 90 miles an hour.'" *Daring Aviator Flies under Local Bridge*, Simpsons' Daily Leader, Kittanning, Pennsylvania, April 22, 1921, William H. Cramer Collection (private), courtesy of Mr. and Mrs. R. Duxbury (hereinafter referred to as Cramer Collection): "We would certainly like to know just what your minimum rate would be to come up here and stage the [parachute] drops from our plane. Kindly quote prices for one, two and three drops on a single trip up here." Letter from G.A. Parsons, Waterbury [Connecticut] Aviation Co., Inc., to Parker Cramer, Cramer Collection; Cramer's standard stunt flying contract in 1921 called for the "First party [Cramer] to furnish his own airplane and give a thirty minute exhibition of stunt flying (the said thirty minutes to include the necessary climbing for altitude) . . . and agrees to give [the party of the second part] 25% of any and all passenger flight money received by him . . . such flight rates to be fifteen dollars for straight flight of approximately ten minutes duration." Cramer Collection.

75. In the single year of 1975, by way of comparison, 80,000 scheduled flights were made over the North Atlantic, ferrying 8,782,176 passengers and more than half a million tons of cargo. Per David Mondey, *The International Encyclopedia of Aviation* (New York: Crown Publishers, 1977), p. 260.

76. Parker D. Cramer, *A Northern Air Route to Europe*, (1931), p. 6, Cramer Collection.

77. Mondey, *International Encyclopedia of Aviation*, p. 261. Even though Cramer surveyed this route three times—and twice before Lindbergh's survey flight—the encyclopedias mention Lindbergh's sole flight. As one of Cramer's friends wrote to him in 1931: "It is unfortunate, but true, that anything he [Lindbergh] does seems to be entirely new and publicly accepted, no matter how old or how skeptical the project." Ernest Jones to Parker Cramer, June 12, 1931, Cramer Collection.

78. Cramer, *A Northern Air Route*, p. 4, Cramer Collection.

79. Gies, *The Colonel of Chicago*, p. 119.

80. John T. McCutcheon, "One Angle of the *Bowler's* Flight," *Chicago Tribune*, July 5, 1929, p. 1.

81. *Chicago Tribune*, June 30, 1929, pp. 1–2.

82. *Ibid.*, p. 2.

83. *Ibid.* The notion that the flight was McCormick's idea is dismissed by a November, 1928, article by Professor William H. Hobbs, director of the University of Michigan's Greenland Expedition, who helped rescue Cramer and Hassel from the ice cap in September, 1928, that claims: "The flight is to be repeated next summer, but this time with an amphibian plane. . . ." See "The Third University of Michigan Greenland Expedition," by William H. Hobbs, The Michigan *Alumnus*, Vol. 35, No. 5 (November 3, 1928), p. 4, Cramer Collection.

84. *Ibid.*, p. 1.

85. *Chicago Tribune*, June 29, 1929, p. 1.

86. *Ibid.*, pp. 1–2. The story went on: "In their flight, Gast and Cramer will face much that is unknown and in addition to mapping an air route they will endeavor to contribute scientific data on the topography of the country over which they fly.

"Bearing northeast from Milwaukee, the Europe-bound *Bowler* will fly to Sault Ste. Marie, where the plane will be cleared from Canadian customs. This formality completed, the ship will continue on to Cochrane, Ontario, and land on Remi Lake, an Ontario forestry control station, 640 miles from Milwaukee. Then the ship will pick up supplies and push on 197 miles to Rupert House on the Rupert River. There at the Hudson Bay Indian trading post, the *Bowler* and its crew will anchor for the first night.

"The second day the first stop will be 816 miles farther along the great circle, on the north tip of Labrador. There at Port Burwell, on Cape Chidley in Ungava Bay, the flyers will drop down for gas. Port Burwell has a radio station, whose call letters are VCH, but if the *'Untin' Bowler*'s radio lives up to expectations, its services will not be needed.

"Port Burwell is up north of the fog country on one of the ribs of the world where they have real daylight savings. The sun shines 20 hours a day, so the *Bowler* and its crew will fly on to Mount Evans, skirt the east coast of Baffinland over Cape Walsingham, visit Holstenborg, capital of north Greenland, and fly up the Stromfjord to Mount Evans, where they will land in protected water and spend the night at Hobbs' camp.

"For more than 500 miles on the second day the flyers will look down on great seas of broken ice and icebergs. There are no towns along this stretch and only a few thousand Eskimos in the country.

"The third flying day will find the *Bowler* heading across the great ice cap of Greenland, over which no plane has ever flown. . . The first settlement is 375 miles from Mount Evans and is called Angmagsallik. There is a radio station there with the call O3L, but the *Bowler* will merely dip down to salute it, continuing on 469 miles to Reykjavik, Iceland's big town.

"Pushing onward the next day, the *Bowler* will follow the coast of Iceland for 175 miles and then cut across the sea to Thorshaven in the Faroe Islands. By skirting the Iceland coast, the water jump will be held down to less than 300 miles. This jump will offer the greatest hazard of the trip, for it crosses the gulf stream, and where the gulf stream flows flyers catch fogs. Furthermore, the Faroe Islands are only tiny dots in the ocean and do not offer a very large target to shoot at. To offset this danger the *Bowler* will be flying over a stretch of water comparatively free of large ice, and there will be numerous fishing boats and trawlers—probably the first the flyers will see—plying along the banks.

"If the *Bowler* makes the Faroe Islands on a bee line there will be no stop at Thorshaven. Glad to be away from the land of the iceberg factories, the flyers will head on toward the Shetland Islands across 210 miles of open water and on to Bergen, Norway, where they probably will pass the fourth night.

"On the fifth morning they will fly 190 miles to Oslo, down Kattegat Strait between the Baltic and the North Sea. From Oslo they will continue 302 miles to Copenhagen, Denmark, and from there to Berlin, 220 miles across land and water, to complete one-half of their journey."

87. *Chicago Tribune*, July 1, 1929, p. 3.

88. Agreement between Robert R. McCormick and Robert H. Gast and Parker D. Cramer, June 29, 1929, Cramer Collection.

89. *Chicago Tribune*, July 3, 1929, p. 1.

90. *Chicago Tribune*, July 4, 1929, p. 3.

91. *Ibid.*, p. 1. Cramer wrote that they flew "through a dozen rain storms" and saw "plenty of lakes most of the course" on the way to Remi Lake. Log of the *'Untin' Bowler*, July 3, 1929, Cramer Collection.

92. *New York Times*, July 4, 1929, p. 2.

93. *Chicago Tribune*, July 6, 1929, p. 1. Cramer wrote in the log: "Continue on to point about 100 miles south of Great Whale. Fog from ice . . . go down to fly over trees but gets thick. Turn around and fly along shore to Rupert House. . . ." Log of the *'Untin' Bowler*, July 4, 1929, Cramer Collection.

94. *Ibid.* To operate the radio in the small aft cabin of the S-38, Cramer reeled out a trailing wire to enhance reception of transmissions from Chicago. "The length of the antenna required for the transmitter is—two pieces of wire each 28 feet from transmitter to far end. If ground is used a little more will be used. Set may be operated very well on the ground or in the water as long as port motor runs. SHOULD THE PORT MOTOR CUT OUT THE GENERATOR MAY BE SHIFTED OVER TO THE STARBOARD MOTOR IN A VERY FEW MINUTES . . . Reception is . . . carried on using the trailing wire which may be let out all the way or just a few feet as desired. Normally reception could be carried on with about ten feet—however more antenna will bring more signal strength and perhaps a little more engine noise . . . If a landing was made on ground, ice or water the trailing wire could be pulled out and hung on one of the lower wings temporarily with a spare insulator. The antenna reel is easily taken off and wire and fish can be dropped in easily by taking out two screws. See 'Instructions for Operation of Radio on Board the *'Untin' Bowler*,' " Cramer Collection.

95. Log of the *'Untin' Bowler*, July 4, 1929, Cramer Collection.

96. *Ibid.*, July 5, 1929.

97. *Chicago Tribune*, July 5, 1929, p. 2.

98. *Chicago Tribune*, July 7, 1929, p. 1.

99. *Chicago Tribune*, July 10, 1929, pp. 1–2.

100. *Ibid.*, p. 2.

101. *Ibid.*

102. *Chicago Tribune*, July 11, 1929, p. 2. Well, not quite. A receipt in Shorty Cramer's notes shows that Chesley Ford, the factor at Port Burwell, collected $200 in wages for a dozen local Eskimos, at the rate of $4 a day and $5 a night. Tommy, Sr., Henry, and Paulus earned the most, each collecting $16 for four days work. See "Wages for Transportation of Gas per Following Natives," July 13, 1929, Cramer Collection.

103. *Chicago Tribune*, July 13, 1929, p. 2.

104. *Chicago Tribune*, July 15, 1929, pp. 1–2. Wood writes that the S-38 slipped into the sea, perforce, it sank. A slightly different eyewitness account was provided by Corporal F. McInnes, the Royal Canadian Mounted Policeman in charge of the Port Burwell detachment. McInnes wrote that the S-38 "finally drifted out into Ungava bay and was seen to settle down on its tail, leaving only its nose protruding above the water, where is [sic] was held to the ice by the mooring anchor. The aero-boat disappeared in that position in the gathering dusk, and no doubt soon sank to the bottom of the bay." Dominion of Canada, *Report of the Royal Canadian Mounted Police for the Year ended September 30, 1929* (Ottawa, 1930), p. 88. McInnes, unlike Wood, does not claim to have actually seen the S-38 sink.

105. Parker D. Cramer, Winging Past the Midnight Sun (unpublished manuscript, 1931), pp. 14–15, Cramer Collection.

106. Robert Wood, "*Bowler* Fliers Start Home by Ship," *New York Times*, July 29, 1929, p. 3.

Notes, Epilogue

107. Jerome Edwards, *The Foreign Policy of Col. McCormick's Tribune, 1929–1941* (Reno: University of Nevada Press, 1971), pp. 45–46.

108. Cramer, *Winging Past the Midnight Sun*, p. 16.

109. Ernest Jones to Parker Cramer, June 12, 1931, Cramer Collection. Another friend wrote to Cramer that: "People don't seem to take to this sort of thing like they did a year ago, and it is no doubt due to the number of flights made in the past year which have been given so much cheap publicity, and also, because of the financial depression." Jack Ford to Parker Cramer, February 2, 1931, Cramer Collection. There is also a peculiar post-script from a letter from Prof. Hobbs at the University of Michigan, written to Cramer after the latter returned from Antarctica, which reads: "If you are planning to see Col. McCormick better see me first. I have much to talk over with you." William H. Hobbs to Parker Cramer, April 1, 1930, Cramer Collection.

110. American Consulate General in Glasgow, Scotland, to the Secretary of State, August 28, 1931, Cramer Collection.

111. Igor Alexis Sikorsky. *The Technical History of Sikorsky Air-*

craft and its Predecessors (Since 1909) (Stratford, CT: Sikorsky Aircraft Corporation, May, 1966), p. 79, Archive and Historical Resource Center, United Technologies Corporation, East Hartford, CT. See also: Edward R. Armstrong, *America-Europe via North Atlantic airways over the Armstrong seadrome system of commercial ocean transit by airplane*. Wilmington, Delaware: The Armstrong Seadrome Development Co., 1927.

112. Sikorsky, *Winged-S*, p. 185.

Bibliography

Unpublished Papers and Archival Records

William H. Cramer Collection, currently in possession of Cramer family, Bloomington, Minnesota.

Alexander Forbes Papers, Rare Books Department, Count Way Library, Harvard University Medical School Library, Cambridge, Massachusetts.

Alexander Forbes Labrador Collection, Gray Herbarium Library, Harvard University, Cambridge, Massachusetts.

Sikorsky Aircraft Flying Boat Records, Archive and Historical Resource Center, United Technologies Corporation, East Hartford, Connecticut.

Sikorsky Aircraft, *Erection Instructions for Sikorsky-Amphibion Airplane* (January 14, 1930), NNIL Branch, National Archives, Washington, D.C.

Test of the Sikorsky Amphibian S-38, War Department, Air Corps Technical Report, Serial No. 3036 (Wright Field, Dayton, Ohio, March 18, 1929), National Air & Space Museum Archives (NASMA).

Robert W. Wood Collection, Polar Archives, Scientific, Economic, and Natural Resources Branch, National Archives, Washington, D.C.

Published Documents

Dominion of Canada. *Report of the Royal Canadian Mounted Police for the Year Ended September 30, 1929* (Ottawa, 1930), National Archive of Canada, RCMP File, RG-18.

Sikorsky Aviation Corporation. *Instructions for the Maintenance and Care of the Sikorsky Amphibion Type S-38* (Bridgeport, Connecticut, n.d.), NASMA.

Sikorsky Manufacturing Corporation. *Sikorsky Amphibion S-38* (College Point, Long Island, New York, 1928; prepared by Brearley Service of New York), NASMA.

Sikorsky, Igor Alexis. *The Technical History of Sikorsky Aircraft and its Predecessors (Since 1909)* (Stratford, Connecticut: Sikorsky Aircraft Corporation, May, 1966), Archive and Historical Resource Center, United Technologies Corporation, East Hartford, Connecticut.

National Advisory Committee for Aeronautics. *The Sikorsky Twin-Engined Amphibian Type S-38 Model 1928*, Aircraft Circular No. 79 (Washington, August, 1928), NASMA.

Correspondence and Interviews

Dr. William Carlson, 1988; Susan Duxbury, 1991–92; Capt. Robert Hanley, 1988; Harry Hleva, 1988–89; Ralph B. Lightfoot, 1986–89.

Articles

Capelotti, P. J. "Ralph Lightfoot's Half-Century in the Air," *Rhode Island*, July, 1987.

Capelotti, P. J. "Aeronautical History at Kingston," University of Rhode Island *Alumni Quarterly*, Vol. LXIII, No. 1, Summer, 1985.

Capelotti, P. J. "An Experiment in Flight," University of Rhode Island *Pacer*, May 3, 1984.

Douglas, Alec. "The Nazi Weather Station in Labrador," *Canadian Geographic*, Vol. 101, No. 6, December 1981/January 1982.

Ellis, Frank H. "Air Pioneers Over Greenland," *Flying*, Vol. 57, No. 6, December, 1955.

Gould, Richard. "The Archaeology of War," in Gould, Richard A., ed. *Shipwreck Anthropology*. Albuquerque: University of New Mexico Press, 1983.

Hobbs, William H. "The Third University of Michigan Greenland Expedition," *The Michigan Alumnus*, Vol. 35, No. 5, November 3, 1928.

"Johnson's Expedition to the Skies," *Johnson Wax Magazine*, Vol. 58, No. 1, Winter 1984–85.

King, Eleanor. "Fieldwork in Brazil: Petrullo's Visit to the Yawalapiti," *Expedition*, Vol. 35, No. 3, 1993.

Lightfoot, Ralph B. "Sikorsky Flying Boats," *American Aviation Historical Society Journal*, Vol. 24, No. 4, Winter 1979.

Mayborn, Mitch, "The Ugly Duckling: Sikorsky's S-38," *American Aviation Historical Society Journal*, Vol. 4, No. 3, Fall 1959.

Mayborn, Mitch, "The Sikorsky S-38 in Australia and the Pacific," *American Aviation Historical Society Journal*, December, 1961.

Neville, Leslie E. "The Sikorsky S-38," *Aviation*, July 28, 1928.

New York Times. "Sikorsky In Plane Falls Into Bay," June 1, 1927.

Petrullo, Vincenzo. "'Among Friends,' Excerpt from *Uni*, an Unpublished Manuscript," *Expedition*, Vol. 35, No. 3, 1993.

Books

Allward, Maurice. *An Illustrated History of Seaplanes and Flying Boats*. New York: Dorset Press, 1988.

Armstrong, Edward R. *The Seadrome Project for Transatlantic Airways, 1943*. Wilmington, Delaware: Seadrome Patents Co., 1943.

Armstrong, Edward R. *America-Europe via North Atlantic airways over the Armstrong seadrome system of commercial ocean transit by airplane*. Wilmington, Delaware: The Armstrong Seadrome Development Co., 1927.

Barry, Jim. *Flying the North Atlantic*. London: B. T. Batsford, 1987.

Barton, Captain Charles. *Howard Hughes and his Flying Boat.* Blue Ridge Summit, Pennsylvania: Aero, 1982.

Bender, Marylin & Selig Altschul. *The Chosen Instrument: Juan Trippe, Pan Am, and the Rise and Fall of an American Entrepreneur.* New York: Simon & Schuster, 1982.

Bleriot, Louis. *Wings Over the Sea: Are Landing Places Necessary for the Commercial Aerial Crossing of the North Atlantic?* Washington, 1936.

Brimm, Daniel J., Jr. *Seaplanes.* New York: Pitman Publishing Company, 1937.

Brock, Horace. *Flying the Oceans: A Pilot's Story of Pan Am, 1935-1955.* New York: J. Aronson, 1983.

Cochrane, Dorothy, et al. *The Aviation Careers of Igor Sikorsky.* Seattle: University of Washington Press, 1989.

Cohen, Stan. *Wings to the Orient: A Pictorial History.* Missoula, Montana: Pictorial Histories Publishing Company, 1985.

Daley, Robert. *An American Saga: Juan Trippe and His Pan American Empire.* New York: Random House, 1980.

Davies, R.E.G. *Airlines of the United States Since 1914.* Washington, D.C.: Smithsonian Institution Press, 1983.

Davies, R.E.G. *Airlines of Latin America Since 1919.* Washington, D.C.: Smithsonian Institution Press, 1984.

Davies, R.E.G. *Pan Am: An Airline and Its Aircraft.* New York: Orion Books, 1987.

Delear, Frank J. *Igor Sikorsky: His Three Careers in Aviation.* New York: Dodd, Mead and Co., 1976.

Dymond, D.P. *Archaeology and History: A Plea for Reconciliation.* London: Thames and Hudson, 1974.

Edwards, Jerome. *The Foreign Policy of Col. McCormick's Tribune, 1929-1941.* Reno: University of Nevada Press, 1971.

Forbes, Alexander. *Northernmost Labrador Mapped from the Air.* New York: American Geographical Society, Special Publication No. 22, 1938.

Forbes, Alexander. *Quest for a Northern Air Route.* Cambridge: Harvard University Press, 1953.

Gandt, Robert L. *China Clipper: The Age of the Great Flying Boats.* Annapolis: Naval Institute Press, 1991.

Gies, Joseph. *The Colonel of Chicago.* New York: E.P. Dutton, 1979.

Glines, C.V., ed. *Polar Aviation.* New York: Franklin Watts, Inc., 1964.

Gould, Richard A. *Recovering the Past.* Univ. of New Mexico Press, 1993.

Gunston, Bill, ed. *The Illustrated Encyclopedia of Propeller Airliners.* London: Phoebus Publishing, 1980.

Hassell, Col. Bert R.J. *A Viking with Wings.* Bend, Oregon: Maverick Publications, 1987.

Holdridge, Desmond D. *Northern Lights.* New York: The Viking Press, 1939.

Holmes, Donald B. *Air Mail, An Illustrated History, 1973-1981.* New York: Clarkson N. Potter, 1981.

Jablonski, Edward. *Seawings: The Romance of the Flying Boats.* Garden City, New York: Doubleday & Co., 1972.

Jackson, Donald Dale. *The Explorers.* Chicago: Time-Life Books Inc., 1983.

Jackson, Ronald W. *China Clipper.* New York: Everest House, 1980.

Johnson, Herbert F., Jr., with Arthur Dailey. *Carnauba Expedition.* Racine, Wisconsin: privately printed, 1936.

Johnson, Osa. *I Married Adventure.* Philadelphia: J. B. Lippincott Company, 1940.

Johnson, Osa. *Last Adventure: The Martin Johnsons in Borneo.* New York: William Morrow & Company, Inc., 1966.

Juptner, Joseph P. *U.S. Civil Aircraft*, Vol. 2. Aero Publishers, Inc., 1964.

Kaucher, Dorothy. *Wings Over Wake.* San Francisco: John Howell, 1947.

Kent, Rockwell. *N by E.* Middletown, Connecticut: Wesleyan University Press, 1978 (reprint of edition published by Brewer & Warren of New York in 1930).

Knott, Captain Richard C. *The American Flying Boat.* Annapolis: Naval Institute Press, 1979.

Mondey, David. *The International Encyclopedia of Aviation.* New York: Crown Publishers, 1977.

Morison, Samuel Eliot. *The European Discovery of America: The Northern Voyages.* Oxford: Oxford University Press, 1971.

O'Neill, Ralph A., with Joseph F. Hood. *A Dream of Eagles.* San Francisco: San Francisco Book Co., 1973.

Sikorsky, Igor I. *The Story of the Winged-S.* New York: Dodd, Mead and Co., 1941.

Solberg, Carl. *Conquest of the Skies: A History of Commercial Aviation in America.* Boston: Little, Brown & Company, 1979.

Stott, Kenhelm W., Jr. *Exploring with Martin and Osa Johnson.* Chanute, Kansas: Martin and Osa Johnson Safari Museum Press, 1978.

Yenne, Bill. *Northwest Orient.* London: Bison Books, 1986.

Index

Will an S-38 Fly Again?

IN THE FINE tradition of stopping the presses so reminiscent of the S-38 era, word arrives at Flying Boat Society HQ in late February, 1995, of an effort to build not one but two flyable S-38s from scratch.

Of course word has circulated countless times in years past, and during my internship at the United Technologies Archive & Historical Resource Center, I personally answered several inquiries from enthusiasts seeking copies of original Sikorsky flying boat plans. We had them, all right, sitting in huge flat heavy wooden crates in a locked room not far from my office. Many times I would look at those stacked boxes and read off the names, bottom to top: S-43, S-42, S-41, S-40, S-38, S-39. Absently, I would wish for a winning lottery ticket, or indulgent millionaire parents, or a suddenly deceased aunt with a legacy, in order to take those crinkled old engineering drawings and have a copy built of each one. (The possibilities seemed endless: Spielberg movies; recreating pioneer flights in the S-38; hopping the South Pacific in a -42; and, my favorite, landing in Hamilton Harbor, Bermuda, in an S-40.)

All these daydreams, like the outside inquiries, came to naught, in the main because of then-standing United Technologies policy not to release copies of the plans because of the liability issue. Should someone actually build a Sikorsky flying boat and, a la Frances Grayson, vanish with or without a trace, the corporate lawyers envisioned waves of irate surviving relatives and their salivating personal injury lawyers descending on United Technologies HQ in Hartford.

But this latest news is deemed reliable because of the track record of the man undertaking the project.

According to the February, 1995, issue of *Sport Aviation*, R. W. "Buzz" Kaplan of Owatonna, Minnesota, retired tool manufacturer and winner of numerous Oshkosh and international awards for his restored floatplanes and amphibians, has formed a company called Born Again Restorations (BAR). The general manager of the new corporation is Dick Andersen, a former co-worker with Kaplan. The company's specific purpose is the construction of two S-38s, the first of which is scheduled to take to the skies in just two years.

The team has obtained a copy of a set of S-38 blueprints from FAA files, and has searched some of the same Sikorsky flying boat files I catalogued in 1988. When I spoke with Dick Andersen in early March he mentioned that the team would like to examine any parts from any original S-38s that may still be in existence. Any S-38 researchers, historians, or aviation archaeologists with knowledge of any such components can reach Dick at the following:

BAR
P. O. Box 274
Owatonna Airport
Owatonna, Minnesota 55060
Phone: (507) 451-8058
Fax: (507) 451-8138

When this first book devoted solely to the S-38 is ready for update and revision around the turn of the century, we hope we will have the pleasure, not only of reading about a complete S-38 reconstruction, but the enjoyment of something that simply does not exist today: color images of an S-38 flying boat in flight.

About the author

P. J. CAPELOTTI holds M.A. degrees in history from the University of Rhode Island (1989) and in anthropology from Rutgers University (1994). His books include *Our Man in the Crimea: Commander Hugo Koehler and the Russian Civil War* (South Carolina, 1991), and his scholarly and popular articles have appeared in *Polar Record, Explorers Journal,* and *Air & Space Smithsonian.* He journeyed to the high Arctic in the summer of 1993 to survey a turn-of-the-century airship hangar and wreck on an island in the Spitsbergen archipelago, and is currently writing his dissertation on the computer-based recording of historic sites in the polar regions, undersea, and in space. His other interests include the transoceanic diffusion of human populations, and how this process interacts with the history of human exploration.

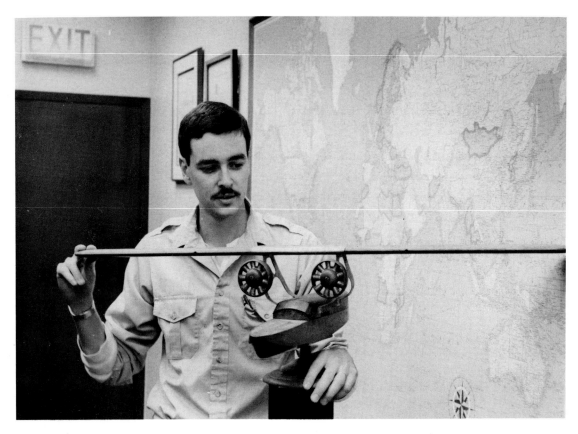

The author with wind tunnel model of Sikorsky S-38, August, 1988. UTC ARCHIVES